Civil War
Weapons and Equipment

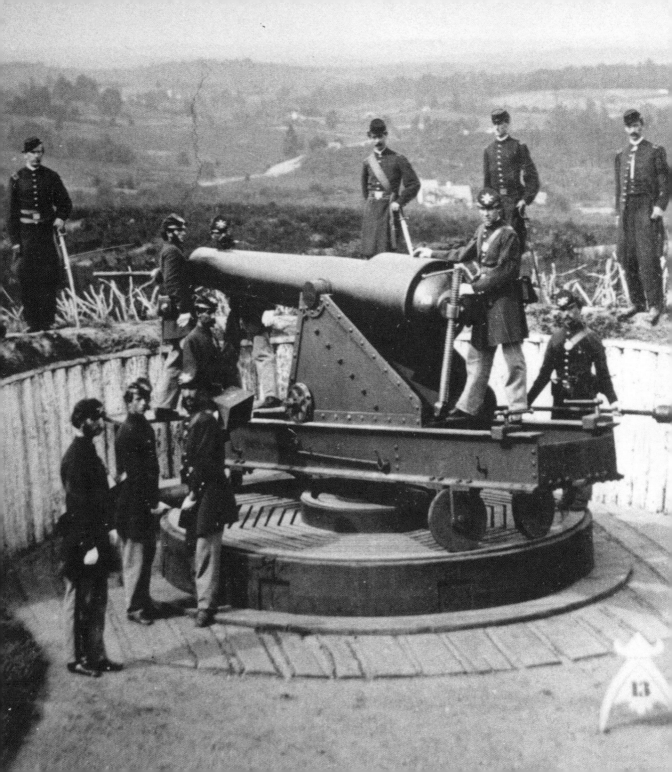

CIVIL WAR
WEAPONS AND
EQUIPMENT

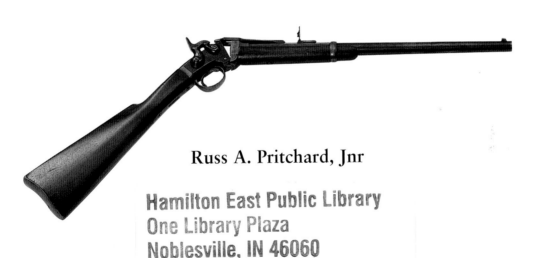

Russ A. Pritchard, Jnr

THE LYONS PRESS

A Salamander Book

Published in the United States by The Lyons Press
Guilford, CT 06437
www.lyonspress.com
An imprint of The Globe Pequot Press

© Salamander Books Ltd., 2003

A member of Chrysalis Books plc

ISBN 1 58574 493 X

1 3 5 7 9 8 6 4 2

The Author
Russ A. Pritchard, Jnr., is a graduate of The Choate School, Wallingford, CT, and Washington and Lee University,
Lexington, Va. He was Executive Director of The Civil War Library and Museum from 1976 until 1995,
and was technical advisor for the acclaimed Civil War trilogy published by Salamander Books, as well as
for four other Salamander titles of American historical interest, and a major contributor to Salamander's
The Civil War Reenactors' Encyclopedia. Retired now, he lives in Tennessee and Mississippi.

Credits
Project Manager: Ray Bonds
Designer: Heather Moore
Technical Assistant: Jennifer Houck
Artifact Photographer: Don Eiler
Reproduction: Anorax Imaging Ltd.
Printed in China

Acknowledgments
The publishers are grateful to the many private collectors and various institutions that have provided artifacts
and/or illustrations shown in this book. They include The Civil War Library and Museum, Philadelphia, Pa.;
The Museum of the Confederacy, Richmond, Va.; the Virginia Historical Society, Richmond, Va.;
West Point Museum, West Point, N.Y.; Gettysburg Museum of the Civil War, Gettysburg, Pa.;
J. Craig Nannos Collection, Philadelphia, Pa.; Eugene Lomas Collection; U.S. Army Ordnance Museum,
Aberdeen Proving Ground, Md.; U.S. Army Quartermaster Museum, Fort Lee, Va.; the Library of Congress.

Additional captions: Page 2: Model 1861 6.4-inch Parrott Rifle at Fort Stevens; one of the fortifications
that surrounded Washington, D.C. Page 3: the Smith breechloading carbine; one of the interesting
patent breech arms spawned by advances in ordnance technology.

Contents

Introduction

*T*HE INTENSE, LONG-ENDURING and growing popular interest in the American Civil War, the first modern war, is a truly fascinating phenomenon. It seems that no conflict in recorded history has so captured the imagination of so many people throughout the world. The reasons for this interest are multi-level and both simple and complex.

One of the primary reasons for this popularity is photography. The current student is able to view an enormous archive of photographic images of the participants, the politicians, commanders, soldiers and civilians, the equipment and battlefields, and the devastation and the dead. Although small numbers of images exist of the War with Mexico, 1845-1848, and the Crimean War, 1853-1856, the American Civil War was the first conflict that was extensively photographically chronicled.

Another important reason for the continuing interest in the war is that it was systematically documented in print with the publication of the *Official Records of the War of the Rebellion, Union and Confederate Armies*, published by the government in 127 volumes with an index and an accompanying atlas of maps, 1880-1901. In addition, there have been hundreds of reminiscences by veterans of both sides. By the time of the Civil War Centennial, 1961-1965, some one hundred thousand volumes on various Civil War topics were in print and since then that number has likely more than doubled. Topics run the gamut from scholarly studies of units and campaigns and serious biographies to somewhat tangential topics such as sex in the war and the conflict as seen through the eyes of the horses of the major protagonists, even cook books. There are new titles and reprints published constantly.

A further reason is the existence and availability in reasonable numbers of an incredible array of Civil War uniforms, arms and accouterments, military materiél culture. The technology of the Industrial Revolution changed the face of warfare forever and these

Left: *A wooden bridge on the Orange and Alexandria Railroad. Transport of troops and supplies by rail greatly enhanced the performance of both armies. Thus disruption and destruction of rail traffic by both sides was an ongoing effort. The United States Construction Corps was developed to repair wooden bridges such as this one in a matter of hours to keep the US Military Railroad running.*

Above: *Nine-button frock coat of a Federal infantry sergeant, with complete set of accouterments including a brown buff leather waist belt with cap box, cartridge box with brown buff sling, cloth-covered metal canteen, haversack, bayonet and scabbard and knapsack.*

Right: *The canteen and haversack were the source of the soldier's sustenance. The canteen, whether tin or wood, was the soldier's constant companion. An prevalent inscription found on veteran's souvenir canteens is "We drank from the same canteen."*

innovations, coupled with the enormous increase in the size of armies at the time, insured the production and survival of large numbers of three-dimensional military objects, those things so avidly collected and studied today. These objects were instantly collectible and many such items were brought home by individual soldiers as trophies and souvenirs. Even during the war exhibits of military paraphernalia appeared at charity fairs in conjunction with fund raising for the war effort. After the war many of these same trophies were donated to local museums or veterans' organizations. Others were preserved by government facilities as examples of obsolete equipment. In the years after the war huge quantities of surplus military materiél were sold at government auction to arms merchants and entrepreneurs who later sold them on to the public.

In previous wars in the United States and overseas, units were dressed in bright, often multi-colored, uniforms to facilitate recognition. Different regiments of the same army wore distinctive uniforms so each could be identified. By the middle of the 19th century the Federal Army had dispensed with turn-back collars and contrasting facings, and had adopted a practical blue uniform and forage cap of martial bearing that was relatively inexpensive and easy to manufacture. Instead of different uniforms to designate branches of service the same basic uniform was worn with branch indicative colored trim and insignia. Interestingly, Union blue and Confederate gray became almost indistinguishable after a few days' march and could be the aegis of subdued uniforms of modern armies. The green uniforms adopted by Berdan's Sharpshooters may be considered one of the forerunners of camouflage.

The corps badges developed during the war were the genesis of unit shoulder patches and DIs, distinctive insignia, as we know them. The stamped or engraved identification pins and disks sold by sutlers to the soldiers were the beginning of dog tags worn now by every soldier. The Model 1858 canteen was the first mass-produced metal canteen in American service and remained the standard for half a century. The shelter half for the individual soldier was the forerunner of the pup tent known to all modern soldiers, and the rubberized ground cloth and poncho were major advancements in personal comfort and shelter for the soldier.

Advances in ordnance were unimaginable, particularly to some older ordnance officers. In 1855 Jefferson Davis, as Secretary of War, had authorized the Army to adopt as its standard shoulder arm a reduced-caliber, parts-interchangeable rifle musket. The longarm was further simplified with the production of the Model 1861 Rifle Musket, and over one million were produced during the war. This rifle was accurate at 300 yards and replaced the smoothbore Model 1842 that was inaccurate at 100 yards. Telescopic long-range sights were in limited use, particularly by Confederate forces, making accurate small arms fire at over 1,000 yards possible in select circumstances.

Fixed ammunition in the form of a metallic rimfire cartridge was perfected just before the war. The Henry and Spencer rifles fired such a cartridge and were the first lever-action, magazine-fed arms used by the military. Compared with the flintlock musket in production just twenty years before, both arms were more than revolutionary. Some dozen distinctly different patent breechloading, metallic-cartridge carbines were issued in various quantities during the war. The revolver had been grudgingly accepted over the single-shot Model 1842 pistol, and Colt and Remington handguns were procured in large numbers. Weapons such as these sounded the death knell of swords and sabers, which hereafter became cumbersome badges of rank relegated to baggage trains in many cases when in the field.

The Ager or Union "Coffee Mill" gun, the Model 1862 Gatling gun, the Billinghurst-Requa battery gun and the Vandenburgh volley gun were all progenitors of the modern day machine gun. While not fully automatic and not used in quantity, they were massed fire

Left: English Whitworth long-range rifles were imported by the Confederacy in limited numbers. This rifle is fitted with a side-mounted Davison telescopic sight with a cross hair reticule. It is documented that mounted men were hit at ranges from 700 to 1,300 yards. Marksmen that used these weapons were the progenitors of snipers utilized so effectively in later wars. One wonders why such sighting devices were not employed with artillery until the 20th century.

Left: One of the wonder weapons of the Civil War. The Spencer Repeating Carbine utilizing weather-resistant self-contained ammunition was more than a step forward in ordnance development. It was a gigantic leap. Ironically, the army lost interest soon after the war was over and the Spencer Repeating Rifle Company filed for bankruptcy in 1869. The plant was sold at auction to the Winchester Repeating Arms Co.

Below: *British civil engineer William Hale made significant improvements to the rockets of his countryman Sir William Congreve by adding small exhaust ports known as tangential vents that made the projectile spin and gave it some semblance of stability. He also developed a better launching device. The United States paid Hale $25,000 for the use for his design and General McClellan is said to have employed a rocket battery during his ill-fated Peninsula Campaign. General Schimmelfenning used them during the Siege of Charleston in 1864 with negligible results, although the Confederates allowed that they did scare their horses.*

weapons and their effect, both physical and psychological, was not lost on the more imaginative military minds of the day.

The Hanes, Ketchum and Raines patent hand grenades foretold of advances in defensive and offensive hand-thrown anti-personnel weapons. Fuzes and fragmentation were not perfected but their advantages in trench warfare were obvious. Such trench warfare was dictated by accuracy of small arms and artillery fire. It did not take long for the soldier to learn that he was safer in the trench, resulting in miles of elaborate trenches and dugouts. Wire entanglements, *chevaux-de-frise*, and *abatis* were employed with considerable success in slowing the approach of opposing forces to trenches.

Artillery made great strides too. While smoothbore artillery was still in use and would remain so almost until the 20th century, rifled field artillery was being developed that greatly increased range and accuracy, while breechloading artillery pieces saw limited field use. Projectile fuzes used in these guns were becoming more reliable. Timed fuzes enabled airbursts, and percussion fuzes allowed ground bursts, both strong incentives for even more overhead cover in trench systems. The segmented shell and the Mallet polygonal cavity shell allowed more uniform fragmentation. Then there were small Coehorn mortars, light enough to be carried by four men; these accompanied the infantry in the assault, giving immediate and mobile fire support. Artillery became more and more an offensive weapon. Hale's patent rocket launcher, though inaccurate, was another embryonic fire support system that developed into recoilless systems in the 20th century. Small, modified artillery rounds with special fuzes were the beginning of modern anti-

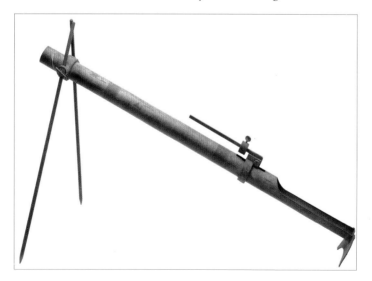

personnel mines and land mine warfare.

Aerial observation became a reality in 1861, soon followed by telegraph communication to the ground. Dr. Thaddeus Lowe became the first chief of the Federal Balloon Corps and designed a converted coal barge to serve as a mother ship, considered by some the first aircraft carrier. This aerial

observation resulted in a Confederate counterpart and even anti-aircraft fire of a sort. Fire direction relayed to mortar batteries on the ground was the first instance of indirect fire control. The use of the telegraph and wig-wag signal flags greatly increased command and control on the battlefield and led to the formation of the Signal Corps.

The ironclad armored ship changed navies forever. John Ericsson's revolving turret and monitor-class ships foretold the end of wooden sailing ships and broadsides. The Brooke rifle and heavy armor-punching projectiles to destroy armored vessels quickly followed. Confederates developed electrically detonated floating mines to block harbors and rivers. They also built submersible craft, one of which, *CSS Hunley*, became the first underwater craft to sink an enemy ship with a torpedo. The little submarine even had a rudimentary snorkel system.

All these imaginative innovations and many others made the Civil War a nightmarish transition from ancient to modern warfare. Some of the tactics developed are still studied today and the origins of many current weapons systems and equipment can be traced to arms and accouterments born during this defining period in military history. It is these historical objects that make up the rich panoply of military materiél culture that are illustrated and discussed in some detail in the following pages.

Russ A. Pritchard, Jr.,
Mississippi, 2003

Above: *The war on shallow inland waterways was the catalyst for the development of a revolutionary armored riverine navy. Some vessels were converted river boats but the backbone of the fleet were the City Class boats – heavily armed, shallow draft paddlewheelers that could navigate the twisting, winding rivers of the south. These boats were effective but service on them was anything but enjoyable. Within the casemate it was dark, cramped and stifling – hardly a pleasant cruise down the river.*

CHAPTER ONE

Uniforms and Insignia

"I have no seat in my pants, the legs are worn out, have had but one pair of socks which are worn out completely, my shirt is literally rotted off me."
(Confederate soldier quoted in *The Liberty Hall Volunteers*, by W. G. Bean)

Below: Chasseur's pattern low crown forage cap of an infantry officer. The curled horn device on the front of the cap indicates the infantry branch and the numeral 10 is the regimental designation. The two subdued strands of quatrefoil and lace specify company grade rank.

*I*T SHOULD COME AS no surprise that many aspects of Federal and Confederate uniforms are remarkably similar. The pattern and cut of many uniform components are almost identical, taking into account allowances for tailoring and available material. The reason for this similarity is that the uniforms of both armies were based on the U. S. Army Uniform Regulations of 1851, as amended in 1858, and Uniform Regulations of 1861.[1] Nevertheless, early volunteers reported for duty wearing a great variety of clothing although, after the first year of the war, uniforms of both combatants were dictated by the need for cost effective simplicity and practicality.

Headgear

By far the most generally recognized piece of Civil War clothing is the forage cap or kepi (from the French *kappe*). This headgear was adopted per General Orders No. 4, War Department, February 26, 1861.[2] The variations of Federal officers' and enlisted men's hats of this pattern are so numerous as to almost defy description.

Federal officers' forage caps were usually of finer quality and made of blue wool cloth with a leather chinstrap attached by brass buttons and leather visor. It had a silk or polished cotton lining, often with the manufacturer's or retailer's name marked in gilt letters in the interior crown, and a wide, thin leather sweat band. Two styles were quite popular and named after the generals who made them so. The

McDowell style had a high, floppy crown and rounded, sharply sloping visor. The McClellan or chasseur style had a much lower crown and squared, slightly angled visor.

General Orders No. 6, War Department, March 13, 1861, stated that all officers would wear respective branch insignia on the front of the forage cap.[3] Some officers followed this regulation, but hats have been noted with branch insignia affixed to the crown, embroidered on the crown, or with no insignia whatsoever. Unit numerals and various corps badges were also worn at the discretion of the officer.

Civilian contractors sold over four million enlisted men's forage caps to the Quartermaster Department, and Army Depots furnished an additional 41,000 caps during the war. Small variations in the height of the crown and width of the visor have been noted in products of the different contractors. Branch of service, company letter, regimental numerical designation and corps badge were worn on the top of the cap rather than at the front. With the exception of the corps badge, all insignia on enlisted men's forage caps was stamped brass.

The forage cap worn by some zouave and chasseur officers was the same basic configuration. Zouave hats were usually made of red wool with gold lace quatrefoil on the top and gold lace strips around the hatband that were rank indicative in the French style. Chasseur hats were standard blue wool with black or gold lace in similar pattern. Chasseur pattern enlisted men's hats were little different from the basic forage cap.

The havelock, a white cloth cover that fitted over the forage cap, and named after British General Henry Havelock, a hero of the Indian Mutiny,[4] is seen in photographs of troops early in the war. These covers supposedly provided some protection from sun and dust on the march, but in fact added to the heat and discomfort of the wearer and were soon discarded.

Another popular but more formal hat was the Pattern 1858 Hat authorized by General Orders No. 3, Adjutant General's Office, March 24, 1858, and appearing in both officer and enlisted man's forms.[5] This black, stiff fur felt hat evolved from the hat that was

Above: From top, McClellan or chasseur's pattern officer's cap with non-regulation application of unit designation numerals without branch insignia directly on the front; artillery officer's McDowell pattern hat with high floppy crown has non-regulation insignia without proscribed black field; red wool forage cap with general officer's gold quatrefoil and lace but no insignia whatsoever.

Above: *The two basic types of enlisted hats: top, blue kepi with infantry horn device; and Regulation Pattern 1858 Hardee hats, one with stamped brass artillery branch insignia and red worsted wool hat cord and brim turned up and pinned with stamped brass eagle badge and plume, the other a non-regulation Hardee hat with infantry horn and blue worsted wool hat cord.*

proscribed for cavalry officers and replaced the Pattern 1851 Hat. It is often referred to as the Hardee hat honoring William J. Hardee (later a Confederate general), who sat on the officers' board that adopted it, or the Jeff Davis hat after Mr. Davis who was Secretary of War at the time of adoption and later President of the Confederate States of America.

The officer's hat was made of the best black felt lined with silk or similar fine fabric and had a wide, thin leather sweatband. The manufacturer's or retailer's name was often embossed in gilt letters in the crown. It had a broad brim, approximately 3¼ inches, with the edge trimmed with black tape, and was turned up on the right side and held to the 6¼ inch high body of the hat by an embroidered eagle badge. Two black ostrich feathers on the left side indicated a company grade officer and three a field grade officer. The body of the hat was encircled by an officer's hat cord and the front of the hat often displayed embroidered branch and unit designation.

The enlisted man's hat was made of lesser grade black felt with a double row of stitching around the brim instead of binding. Branch and unit insignia fabricated of stamped brass were worn on the front of the hat and the body was encircled with a worsted wool hat cord with tassels in branch appropriate color.

These hats were often customized by the wearers and some have been seen without the brim turned up and the body creased from front to rear. One particular variation was referred to as the Burnside Hat[6] after General Ambrose P. Burnside who popularized the style.

The slouch hat was worn by both officers and enlisted personnel. It was a non-regulation, soft-crowned, broad-brimmed dark brown or black hat. The officer's version was usually lined similarly to the Pattern 1858 officer's hat. Many were privately purchased with officers' hat cords and appropriate insignia attached per regulations or the whim of the officer. Those worn by enlisted personnel were very similar, usually of lesser quality, and they exhibited the same individualism with branch and unit insignia. Unquestionably, it was more practical than the forage cap but lacked the martial bearing of the jaunty cap. Field modifications were endless, limited only to the imagination of the wearer. This style was most popular with armies in the Western Theater but did see considerable service in the East.

The chapeau bras or cocked hat was made optional in lieu of the Pattern 1858 Officer's Hat for generals and field grade officers in 1858 after being discontinued in 1851.[7] It was made of beaver with the right side adorned with an intricate rosette of gold lace overlaid with a large silver or gilt eagle. The top of the hat was crowned with ostrich feathers, a magnificent but fragile piece. This hat was used only in garrison for dress occasions and saw no field use.

There was one hat that was branch specific, the Light Artillery shako, sometimes called the Ringgold hat after the officer who formed the first unit of horse artillery in 1838 and was later killed in 1848 in Mexico.[8] It, too, appeared in officer and enlisted configuration. The officer's version had gilt cords and embroidered insignia, while the enlisted model had red wool cords and stamped brass insignia. These intricate cords and lines draped the shoulder and breast of the wearer. Both versions featured a red horse hair plume in a gilt tulip on the top front of the hat. This hat was really impractical for field wear and saw limited use as a dress headgear for mounted artillerymen.

The fez, worn by enlisted men who affected the zouave dress of French colonial troops in North Africa, was strikingly different from all other headgear in the war. While men of Berdan's Sharpshooters wore a bottle green forage cap, and some chasseur units wore French pattern shakos, nothing was as bizarre as the fez with tassel. Most of these were red wool, sometimes worn with a white turban, but some units wore blue or black variations. While colorful, they were impractical and soon discarded in favor of some form of the forage cap by some units.

Officers of the Navy wore a blue wool cap with leather visor and chin strap held by two brass naval buttons, and naval insignia affixed to the front of the hat. Enlisted personnel wore a blue visorless cloth cap much like the flat top dress hat currently in use. Both officers and enlisted men often wore white covers on hats in summer months, and non-regulation straw hats were favored on station in hot climates.

Above: *The Light Artillery Officer's Cap was reintroduced in 1859. This resplendent headgear with gold lace cords that draped across the breast of the uniform coat was not suited for field use and was worn primarily for dress function or garrison duty.*

Below: *The fez was part of the zouave uniform adapted from the dress of French colonial troops in North Africa. Some were worn with an additional turban. Colors varied from regiment to regiment but all were impractical.*

Above: The Marine shako and forage cap both display the unique Marine Corps insignia of curled infantry horn with old English M on a red ground. The shako was used primarily in garrison and on parade. The forage cap was worn in the field and on board ship.

Officers of the small Marine Corps wore a standard forage cap of blue wool with leather visor and chinstrap with Marine Corps buttons, and Marine Corps insignia affixed to the front of the hat. Marine enlisted personnel wore the same type hat for active duty. A dress shako, with stamped brass insignia of Union shield above wreath overlaid with an infantry horn curled around the old English script silver letter M, was worn for dress occasions.[9]

The wide variety of headgear worn early in the war very quickly disappeared, with field-proven styles becoming the norm by the second year. The forage cap and slouch hat became standard throughout the armies, and remained so in modified form until uniform changes at the turn of the century.

Initial lack of uniformity, as well as dependence on local and state sources for uniform cloth, did present one problem at the outset. The color gray had always been popular in the North, and troops from Maine, Pennsylvania, Vermont and Wisconsin arrived at the seat of the war outfitted in uniforms of that color. The War Department asked governors and state officials to discontinue the practice in September 1861 so as to avoid confusion on the battlefield and resultant casualties by friendly fire. This problem was resolved by mid-1862.[10]

Uniform coats

Three basic styles of uniform coats were worn during the war: the sack coat, the frock coat, and shell jacket. All three were made in officer and enlisted configuration. Officers in the East appeared to prefer the frock coat for field use, even during the summer. Toward the end of the war many officers adopted the common sack coat because of obvious comfort and efficiency.

The officer's sack coat appeared in double- and single-breasted styles, with four to six button closure and in various lengths from hip to thigh. Both internal and external pockets have been noted. These coats were all non-regulation, made to order, private purchase items and exhibited considerable diversity. The primary consideration was utilitarian comfort. Certain insignia, color of shoulder strap background and button type and placement were indicative of rank.

The enlisted man's sack coat was authorized for fatigue duties in 1859 and became the uniform of choice of the Union Army by late 1861. Tens of thousands were manufactured during the war at the Cincinnati Arsenal, Schuylkill Arsenal in Philadelphia, and by a number of other private and commercial contractors.[11]

Like the forage cap, the sack coat became a trademark of Billy

Left and below: *Front and back of the trademark coat of the Federal enlisted man. The sack coat with four brass eagle buttons was the basic uniform coat for troops in the eastern and western theaters during most of the war. It was functional and inexpensive.*

Left: *General Officer's Pattern 1851 frock coat with black velvet collar and cuffs. The placement of staff officer's buttons in groups of three indicate rank of major general or above. The buff silk sash is also indicative of general officer rank.*

Yank. The coat was fabricated of loose-fitting, dark blue flannel extending half way down the thigh. It was single-breasted, and had four brass eagle buttons and an interior breast pocket. Most coats were lined but some were not. Non-commissioned rank and branch of service was indicated by color of chevrons on both sleeves. The sack coat was inexpensive, easy to manufacture and practical, the ideal military garment, and most were worn out in service. The pattern continued in use well into the 1870s.[12]

The Pattern 1851 officer's frock coat was made of dark blue wool of varying quality, was lined with polished cotton or silk and had a skirt that extended from two-thirds to three-fourths of the distance from the top of the hip to the bend of the knee. There were generally two interior pockets within the lining of the rear of the skirt and one interior pocket in the left breast. The coat was double-breasted for general and field grade officers and single-breasted for company grade officers. General officers' coats usually had black velvet collars and cuffs. Staff officers' buttons for major generals and above were arranged in two rows of nine buttons in groups of three. Brigadier generals had two rows of eight buttons arranged in groups of two. Field grade officers had two rows of seven buttons each. All company grade officers had one row of nine buttons. Rank and branch of service were additionally designated by shoulder straps in the field, or epaulets for full dress, bearing rank devices on branch specific color backgrounds.[13]

Enlisted men were authorized a nine-button, blue wool, single-

Below: *Front and back of the Pattern 1851 double-breasted frock coat for field grade officers, with two rows of seven buttons. The rank devices were worn directly on the shoulder so as to be less conspicuous but the non-regulation wearing of the Corps Badge on the breast would have made an obvious target.*

Left: *Front and back of the Pattern 1858 enlisted artilleryman's single-breasted, nine-button frock coat. Branch is indicated by the narrow red welt around the collar and cuffs. Garrison and heavy artillery units typically wore frock coats of this type.*

Below: *Short shell jacket of an officer of a zouave regiment. The coat has a velvet collar and gold lace galloons on cuffs and bottom edge but no rank devices on the shoulders. Officers were allowed almost unlimited latitude in cut and designating devices of their privately purchased uniforms.*

breasted frock coat in 1858 that was almost identical to the previous patterns of 1854 and 1855.[14] The coat had a dark polished cotton lining, a skirt that extended one-half the distance from the top of the hip to the bend of the knee, and stand up collar that hooked at the neck. Pocket placement was the same as officers' coats. Brass scale epaulets were worn on the shoulders for dress functions. The collar and cuffs were piped with cord or welt in branch of service color. These frock coats were relegated to garrison duty by many units in favor of the sack coat, but some regiments, such as those in the Iron Brigade, proudly wore their long coats in the field.

The officer's shell jacket appeared in both single- and double-breasted configuration. Rank and branch of service were distinguished as noted for frock coats, although some of these jackets had additional galloons on

Above: *Pattern 1863 New York National Guard shell jacket. State troops often wore uniforms that suited their quartermaster's interpretation of regulations. The buttons are New York State Seal buttons, and note that cuffs, collar, epaulets and all edges are piped in branch of service color.*

the sleeves with the number of strands rank indicative. Most were waist length but some have been noted slightly longer. Some single-breasted jackets had nine to twelve buttons. These jackets seem to have been worn mostly by mounted officers of all branches and were authorized stable jackets for mounted artillery and cavalry.[15]

The shell jacket was worn by enlisted personnel of the artillery, cavalry, some state troops and other specialized units. Artillery and cavalry shell jackets were of the same 1854-1855 pattern.[16] The 1861 Regulations stated that they would be made of dark blue cloth with one row of twelve small brass buttons and stiff stand-up collar hooked at the neck. The collar, cuffs and all edges were piped with three-eighths inch wide tape in the color of branch of service. Brass scale epaulets were worn on the shoulders for dress functions but not worn in the field. The jacket was supposed to be lined with white flannel but a variety of colored fabrics have also been observed.

Many volunteer artillery and cavalry units came into Federal service with their own state issue interpretations of these regulation patterns, exhibiting subtle variations. There also existed some very few dragoon and mounted riflemen's shell jackets in the early months of the war. The only difference was color of the branch of service tape trim. Musicians of these branches wore the same shell jacket with the addition of appropriate colored tape in the form of a plastron on the breast. New York State 1861 and 1863 issue shell jackets were another variation of this pattern.[17] These jackets had cloth epaulets and a belt loop on the left side. The collar, epaulets and later belt loop and cuffs were sometimes trimmed in branch of service color. The Veteran Reserve Corps also wore a shell jacket of sky blue kersey with dark blue tape trim in the style of the artillery and cavalry jackets, with the addition of epaulets.[18]

Uniforms of officers and enlisted men of units that wore zouave dress were truly extraordinary. Many of the officers' coats were standard frock coats, sometimes with unit specific trim. Other officers wore the dark blue shell jacket with sleeves adorned with galloons. A few wore the zouave jacket with appropriate officer rank attached. The enlisted uniform jacket was based on that worn by the elite French North African colonial units. Almost all had the

Left: *The short jacket with integral vest adorned with intricate piping or tape of contrasting color was typical of zouave dress. The sleeves bear the chevrons of a first sergeant. The uniform of each regiment had subtle distinctions and this particular uniform was worn by the 23rd Pennsylvania Infantry, Birney's Zouaves.*

Below: *Pennsylvania state issue cavalry shell jacket of a sergeant of the 6th Pennsylvania Cavalry, Rush's Lancers. Considerable effort was made to conform to regulations but cut and tape trim are distinctly different. Plaid and multi-colored linings were distinctly non-regulation but actually not common.*

decorative device known as tombeau[19] on each breast and the collarless, short, close-fitting jacket did not button but had an integral vest worn with the coat. Some tombeaux were bright red or yellow on the blue jacket.

These jackets, along with other striking pieces of zouave dress, made the soldier so attired a handsome target. There were fewer than two-dozen regiments that affected some variation of zouave dress during the war.[20] Some units opted for less conspicuous Union blue at the first opportunity, but others wore their zouave finery throughout the war.

Somewhat less opulent were the chasseur coats, copied from those worn by French Light Infantry. These were worn by some Massachusetts, New York and Pennsylvania units and were made of dark blue cloth, and were slightly flared and longer than the shell jacket but not as long or shapeless as the sack coat. Most had epaulets, belt loops and colored piping and were lined with dark polished cotton or similar fabric. Some ten thousand were actually imported from France.[21]

The Pattern 1851 Cloak Coat was worn by officers of all ranks and continued in service until replaced in 1872. The coat was made of dark blue cloth with black silk cord on all edges and closed by four black silk frog buttons on the breast. Galloons of the same material on the sleeve were rank indicative.[22] Officers were also authorized to wear enlisted overcoats to blend with the troops.[23] Such use is seen with or without appropriate rank affixed.

The Pattern 1851 Enlisted Overcoat was issued to mounted and dismounted troops. The foot overcoat was made of a blue-gray cloth, and was single-breasted with brass buttons and stand-up collar and cape that fell to the elbow. The mounted overcoat was made of the same cloth, but double-breasted with brass buttons and stand-up collar and cape that fell to the cuff.[24]

Vests

Vests are apparent in many period photographs of officers and enlisted men yet there is no mention of them in any regulations. It was custom that dictated that the shirtfront would not be seen.[25] Thus, those soldiers who chose to wear the coat unbuttoned resorted to the private purchase of a variety of vests. Most were the same blue color and material as the coat, with brass buttons, but buff wool and white linen specimens have also been noted.

Above: *Enlisted man's mounted overcoat. The cape came almost to the cuff, somewhat longer than the dismounted overcoat. Such coats were warm and serviceable and officers often wore them without rank insignia so as to be less conspicuous to Confederate sharpshooters.*

Naval and Marine coats

Naval officers' regulation coats were made of blue cloth, were double-breasted, and had brass buttons and shoulder strap and cuff rank designation. Lining, pocket arrangement and tailoring were generally the same as Army frock coats. Contemporary photography depicts a wide variety of uniforms, single-breasted sack coats with various button arrangements, white linen sack coats[26] and other obviously non-regulation, private purchase coats. This is particularly true of officers on station in southern climates.

Naval petty officers were known to have worn a blue cloth double-breasted shell jacket, with rating badge on the left sleeve at the elbow for dress occasions.[27] The blue cloth pullover seaman's frock with silk kerchief was standard, although a summer white cotton frock with blue facings was also used.[28]

Marine officers' regulation coats were also made of blue cloth, double-breasted, with brass buttons unique to their service and with distinctive quatrefoil shoulder boards. Marine enlisted personnel wore a standard dark blue single-breasted frock coat but with red piping at the collar and branch specific buttons. In 1859, Marines aboard seagoing vessels were authorized a blue flannel fatigue sack rather than the frock coat.[29]

Trousers

Officers' trousers, like other pieces of their uniform, were private purchase items, the product of a tailor or military outfitter. Quality varied depending on the talents of the tailor and the individual officer's pocketbook. General Order 108 dated December 16, 1861, stipulated sky blue kersey for all line officers and the same dark blue wool cloth used in coats for all other officers.[30] This change met mixed acceptance, and photographs depict many officers other than staff in dark blue trousers throughout the war.

The two basic types of officers' trousers were those for foot officers and those for mounted officers. Trousers for dismounted officers were usually not lined. There was a watch pocket in the waistband and two pockets, one on each hip, either of side seam or mule ear type. Those for mounted officers had a reinforced or double thickness seat and leg inseam, and there were often foot straps at the cuff to hold the trouser leg down to the boot when mounted. Some mounted officers' trousers were also fully or partially lined with

Above: *Marine Corps personnel wore an overcoat cut very similar to the mounted overcoat of the Army but it was dark blue rather than sky blue and had a detachable cape. The brass buttons bore the Marine Corps device. This pattern remained in service well into the 1870s.*

Right: *General and staff officers' trousers were dark blue wool, the same material used in coats. General officers' trousers were devoid of any trim but some staff officers had a thin welt of gold lace down the outside seam of their trousers. All had metal or bone button fly closure and buttons for suspenders.*

Far right: *Sky blue trousers for all regimental officers. This particular trouser was for an infantry officer, as indicated by the dark blue welt on the outside seam of the leg. Other branches of service were indicated by appropriate branch of service color. Mounted trousers had reinforced seats and leg inseams.*

muslin or similar fabric and had the same pocket arrangement as previously described. Trousers had metal, bone or porcelain buttons for fly closure, and buttons for suspenders on the waistband, a cotton waistband lining, adjustable belt rear vent closure and no rear pockets or loops for a waist belt.

All officers' trousers, with the exception of those of general officers which were unadorned, had a one-eighth inch staff or branch of service color welt let into the outside seam of the leg.[31]

Besides the two general styles there were also trousers that varied in color and cut for officers of distinctive zouave units and some state units.

Enlisted men's trousers

Trousers for enlisted personnel, like those for officers, were found in mounted and dismounted patterns. Federal and State facilities or civilian contractors made almost all of these trousers and most were serviceable but of lesser quality than those for officers. All trousers were made loose-fitting with the cuff well spread over the boot.

Dismounted men's trousers were usually unlined and had metal, bone or porcelain buttons for fly closure and suspenders. Pocket arrangement was the same as for officers' trousers. The seat and inside of the trouser leg were reinforced for mounted troops. General Order No. 108, previously cited, stipulated that all enlisted personnel except those of the Ordnance Branch would wear sky blue kersey trousers. Ordnance troops retained the dark blue pattern.

Non-commissioned officers had a worsted lace stripe of branch of service color sewn on the out side seam of the leg. Sergeants' stripes were one and one-half inches wide and those for a corporal were one-half inch wide.[32]

Zouave trousers were actually pantaloons that came only just below the knee and were secured by gaiters or jambieres worn with this uniform. Many of these garments were cut very full while others were tailored more like conventional trousers. Some of the pantaloons were bright red, others shades of blue. Combined with other pieces of zouave apparel, these trousers made the soldier a resplendent spectacle on the battlefield.

Below left: *Sky blue kersey dismounted trousers for enlisted personnel. These trousers were usually unlined and very rough on the legs without long underwear.*

Below center: *Rear view of enlisted dismounted trousers showing full cut, adjustable rear vent closure and metal suspender buttons on waist band.*

Below right: *Full cut pantaloons with red welt trim of the 9th New York Infantry, Hawkins' Zouaves. The legs of the trousers came just below the knee and were tucked into special leggings.*

The trousers of Navy and Marine officers were standard dark blue cloth without any unique or branch specific details. Buttons and pocket arrangement were the same as other officers' trousers.

Naval enlisted ranks wore a trouser unique to naval personnel, with bell bottom legs and bib button front closure.[33] Dark blue wool and white cotton trousers were worn dependent on season or climate. Marine enlisted men were authorized sky blue kersey trousers in 1859, very similar to those worn by Army troops.

Shirts

Shirts were considered under-garments, much the same as underwear. Vests were worn to cover them when the coat was worn unbuttoned or with the lapels buttoned back. All were a pullover pattern, often of coarse wool or flannel and cut very full. Colors varied from shades of white and gray to dark blue, and many civilian shirts of plaid and striped designs were worn when issue items were unavailable or when received from home. Most had two to four bone buttons at the neck

Right: Standard pattern wool or flannel pullover shirt. These undergarments varied greatly in color, had no collar and were always cut very full. Most were either government or state issue obtained under contract, although many were brought or sent from home. Most were worn out in service.

Far right: Linen shirt, probably that of an officer. Like other pieces of officer uniform, shirts were private purchase and officers bought what they could afford. Often a stiff collar and cravat were worn with this type of shirt, with the uniform collar open. Civilian shirts frequently had one or two pockets.

and one on each cuff. There were no pockets in military contract shirts but many civilian shirts had one or two. Government contractors, state and local sources, and private purchase provided shirts allowing considerable individuality.

The leather neck stock was a regulation item for officers and enlisted men. It was thought such a device would keep the soldier's head up and give him a more martial bearing. It was little more than a band of leather with a small buckle worn under the collar. Most were left in garrison or lost quickly in the field. Officers and lower ranks did wear cravats or ties on many occasions, as evidenced by contemporary photographs, but it is doubtful if such finery lasted long on the march.

Footwear

Mounted personnel, regardless of rank, usually wore high leather boots. Officers' boots were privately purchased and depended solely on the taste and requirements of the individual. Some were dragoon style that came over mid-thigh, others just over the knee, and some to the top of the calf of the leg. Enlisted men were issued heavy, rigid Wellington Pattern boots that extended to the top of the calf.[34]

Below: Most enlisted mounted personnel wore issue Wellington boots. They were heavy and sturdy and some were worn by officers and dismounted personnel because of their serviceability although they were not designed for a long march. Spurs were issued to mounted troops but many seem to have been quickly lost.

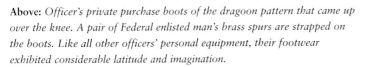

Above: Officer's private purchase boots of the dragoon pattern that came up over the knee. A pair of Federal enlisted man's brass spurs are strapped on the boots. Like all other officers' personal equipment, their footwear exhibited considerable latitude and imagination.

Left: Pattern 1851 Jefferson bootee, the standard issue shoe of the Federal foot soldier. Numerous contractors manufactured this shoe, and quality did vary. Most had metal plates attached to heel and toe to extend serviceability and, by and large, they were comfortable on the march and much liked by the men.

27

Foot soldiers wore the Pattern 1851 Jefferson Brogan, the standard army shoe,[35] made of tanned leather with the rough side out. The top of the boot extended over the ankle and laced with four eyelets. Most had metal plates attached to the squared toe and heel to extend serviceability of the shoe. Sizes ran from 5 to 12. Regulations required brogans to be blackened and bootblack was available from the unit sutler. The quartermaster was the source of these shoes until the huge expansion of the Army dictated by the war. The government was forced to contract with civilian supply sources to meet demand, with initial mixed results. Some early war reports stated that brogans lasted less than two weeks due to poor material and fabrication. Fortuitously, the prewar shoe industry was well established in Northern states and war profiteering was brought under control.

A surprising number of shoes were imported from England, and fine English brogans captured on blockade runners and from Confederate soldiers exist. Some canvas-topped civilian camp or leisure time shoes were also worn.[36]

Branch of service insignia

Officers and enlisted men wore branch of service insignia on hats as proscribed by regulations. Officers' branch devices were of higher quality than those of enlisted men, although the devices were the same form: the curled horn for infantry, crossed cannon for artillery, crossed sabers for cavalry, turreted castle for engineers, and flaming bomb for ordnance. The officers' devices were fashioned of gold embroidered thread on a black velvet ground, or stamped brass to simulate embroidery affixed to a black ground.[37] Enlisted insignia was die stamped sheet brass. A great many variations of all have been noted. Naval officers wore hat insignia that was both branch of service and rank or specialty indicative. No official enlisted hat insignia are known. Marine officers and enlisted men wore a hat insignia of a curled infantry horn surrounding the letter M.[38]

Buttons of the officers' coats were also branch indicative. Field grade and company grade officers' coats often had eagle buttons with the letter A, C or I indicating artillery, cavalry or infantry branch of

Below: *Officers' branch of service and regimental designation insignia vary considerably. Regulations specified branch be indicated by a device on a black velvet ground, the whole affixed to the front of the hat. In this case it is the curled infantry horn. The regimental designation is the numeral 13 within the curl.*

Below: *Regulation artillery officer's hat insignia. The numeral 4 is mounted on a red ground, the branch color of artillery, which makes the device all the more interesting. Some such insignia were not mounted on any ground but affixed directly to the cap.*

service on the shield on the eagle's breast. Ordnance and engineer officers also wore distinctive buttons. Enlisted men of all branches usually wore generic eagle buttons. Naval and Marine personnel had distinctive device buttons and there were a multitude of state seal buttons worn by volunteers from respective states.

Corps badges

According to some sources, in June 1862 Major General Phillip Kearny ordered officers in his III Corps to affix a two-inch square piece of red flannel on their caps for recognition. After his death the custom was continued in his honor and became so popular that Major General Joseph Hooker instituted a system of corps badges in a circular dated March 21, 1863.[39] The stated purpose was to facilitate the ready identification of units and to prevent any injustice to units accused of poor conduct. Specific shapes were assigned to each corps and specific colors – red, white and blue – for each division within that corps.

The first corps badges were cut from common cloth and affixed to the crown of the forage cap or slouch hat. Officers tended to have finer embroidered corps badges that were private purchase items. As the practice increased in popularity, pin-back metal badges became available from sutlers and jewelers. Badges were made of every material from bone to precious metals and were sometimes inscribed or engraved with the owner's name, unit and battle honors. Contemporary photography provides evidence of alternative locations of unit insignia on the left breast of the coat, regardless of pattern.

Rank devices

An officer's rank was generally indicated by shoulder straps worn on the coat. Straps had a gilt border that surrounded a field of fine velvet or wool in branch of service color, upon which the rank device was affixed.[40] These straps were usually sewn to the coat but some had strings or ribbons that attached through eyelets in the fabric of the coat. More expensive straps or those worn by higher ranks had several rows of gilt cord around the edge. Smith's Patent straps had

Below: *Jeweler-made identification badge. Many officers and enlisted men purchased various stock pattern and custom-designed badges on which were engraved name, unit and, in some cases, battle honors. These badges were worn on the breast of the uniform.*

Below: *Shoulder straps were the primary means of rank identification. The background indicated branch of service, in this case red for artillery. The device on the strap indicated the individual's rank, in this case captain.*

Above: *Epaulets were worn in lieu of shoulder straps on dress occasions in garrison. The rank and branch of service and unit designation were attached to the epaulets. In this rare example, the bar indicates the officer is a 1st lieutenant. The orange ground and numeral indicates the unit is the 2nd Dragoons.*

Right: *Sashes were authorized for all officers and non-commissioned officers. Officers' sashes were silk. This NCO sash is worsted wool. The sash was worn under the waist belt on a day to day basis. When the individual was NCO of the Day the sash was worn over the right shoulder with tassels tied on left hip.*

die-stamped brass edges of simulated embroidery with brass rank insignia.

As the war continued and officer casualties mounted, wearing of rank insignia became more discreet; small insignia only were found on the collar, or on the shoulder without straps, or there was a single rank insignia pinned on the breast. Dress epaulets with rank insignia affixed were worn for parades and formal functions. The size of the gilt fringe of the epaulets also indicated rank.

Naval officers' rank was indicated by both shoulder straps and cuff stripes. There were eight commissioned ranks and, to add to the confusion, there was unique insignia for specialists such as engineers, paymasters and surgeons to distinguish them from line officers.[41]

General officers wore a gilt hat cord with acorn tips on slouch hats while other officers wore a similar black and gilt hat cord. Sashes were also badges of rank. General officers wore a buff silk sash while other officers wore maroon silk sashes, except for surgeons who wore a green silk sash.

Branch of service colors used for trimming and piping of coats and trousers, and rank insignia grounds, were red for artillery, yellow for cavalry, blue for infantry, crimson for ordnance, green for medical, black for general and staff officer, and a darker yellow for engineers.

Non-commissioned officers wore a maroon or dark red worsted wool sword belt sash. Inverted vee sleeve chevrons in branch of service color indicated enlisted rank. Polished brass scale epaulets were worn on the shoulders by enlisted ranks for parade and formal events.

Confederate uniforms

The bureaucracy of the new government of the Confederate States of America emulated the uniform regulations that they were most familiar with, and in

Spring 1861 formulated the *Uniform and Dress of the Army of the Confederate States* and *Uniform and Dress of the Navy of the Confederate States*, based almost entirely upon regulations of Federal counterparts. The major exceptions were initial army uniform style and rank devices and color of naval uniforms.

Current belief is that Nicola Marschall, a Prussian artist, suggested the Austrian uniform to the Uniform Board of Congress. The tunic was double-breasted, gray, with two rows of seven buttons for all ranks, the skirt to reach half way between the hip and thigh. The trousers were light blue for enlisted men and regimental officers and dark blue for higher ranks. Rank insignia on the collar was a modification of the Austrian system. The colored trim and sashes were the same as for the United States Army. The kepi and rank indicative sleeve galloons of the French army were adopted.[42]

The Confederate Navy regulations formulated in early 1861 specified gray uniforms, a radical departure from blue naval uniforms of every other navy in the world.[43]

The Austrian pattern uniform and the gray naval uniform were both unpopular. The Austrian tunic was replaced quickly by the familiar frock coat, although collar and sleeve rank insignia were retained. Naval officers begrudgingly accepted the gray coat and there exist several examples of these coats made in England.

Above: Confederate officer's frock coat: turned-down collar hides rank, but sleeve galloons indicate ranking officer and button placement in groups is applicable to general officer; saber indicates cavalry, but actually he is Col. Montford S. Stokes, 1st North Carolina Infantry, in an example of uniform dictated by personal preference.

31

Above: *General officer's regulation frock coat. The collar bears the rank device of a general officer, three gilt stars on a buff field surrounded by a gilt wreath. The button placement in groups of two also conform to regulations, as does the buff piping on the edge of the coat of Major General John B. Gordon of Georgia.*

One other peculiarity of the Confederate system of uniform supply existed briefly. Initially, the Confederate government was responsible for supplying uniforms only to the 6,000 regular troops authorized. The remaining 100,000 volunteers from various states, the Provisional Army, were responsible for furnishing their own uniforms or being clothed by the respective states, with the central government reimbursing them at the rate of $50.00 per year. This Commutation System did not work and was discontinued in October 1862[44] and, thereafter, the Quartermaster Department furnished uniforms for all armies from a system of depots.

The depot system, supplemental supply by state sources, importation of ready-made uniforms from abroad, captured Federal quartermaster supplies, and clothing furnished by family and local sources at home account for the great variety of Confederate uniforms. Although there was diversity from depot to depot and in different theaters of the war, in general the Confederate army was well uniformed and equipped throughout the war.

Confederate headgear

The authorized kepi was much more popular in the Eastern theater, particularly with officers. Regulations for officers' caps stated that the whole body of the hat would be of branch of service color topped with quatrefoil designating rank and with leather visor and chin strap held by appropriate buttons. Officers purchased their own headgear and tailors had their own interpretation of regulations, so an officer's kepi fabricated to quartermaster specifications was unusual, although many did exist. More often, the body of the hat was encircled by a band of cloth in branch of service color or piped in appropriate color. An inexpensive oilcloth or tarred fabric was often substituted for the leather of the brim. An enormous variety of imported and local buttons were used to hold the chinstrap. Forage caps in the style of the Pattern 1858 of the U.S. Army were also used, with the McDowell type being very popular.[45] Enlisted men's kepis, made of various materials such as wool and cotton jean cloth, were supplied by quartermaster sources throughout the war, the Richmond Depot being a prolific source. Branch colors were specified but such technicalities were often ignored, and caps that were available were issued to those in need regardless of branch of service color.

The havelock was also inflicted upon enthusiastic Confederate volunteers in 1861. They came to the same conclusion as the soldiers in blue and soon discarded them as useless.

Below: *Unusual general officer's forage cap in gray wool with general officer's four strands of gilt lace around the body of the hat, yet the quatrefoil on the crown is only one strand within a non-regulation circle made of one strand.*

Above: *Brigadier John Bankhead Magruder's forage cap not only conformed to regulations in color and trim but exceeded them with the script CSA embroidered within the stylized wreath on the front of his hat, a truly magnificent piece of headgear.*

Below: *The imported French hat with black plume and officer's hat cord bears no other military insignia whatsoever, yet this is the hat of the foremost cavalry leader of the Confederacy, Major General J. E. B. Stuart, another testimonial to individuality.*

Above: Foul weather gear and rain hats were private purchase items. Most Confederate soldiers did have the luxury of such comfort although a small number of raincoats, ponchos and rain hats have survived. This example made of rubberized cloth has a visor and neck protection.

The slouch hat in every form and color imaginable was universally popular with Confederate soldiers, both officers and enlisted ranks, of all armies. It was non-regulation and field modifications were endless. Most of them were private purchase items, often civilian but always practical, the key requirement. Officers sometimes placed officers' hat cords on them and some wore plumes, as exemplified by General Stuart. Reinforced or unreinforced wide or narrow brims were turned up or down, pinned in various manners with state related badges at the whim of the wearer. Some were imported with fine silk lining and others were common straw hats from the farm. Branch of service insignia in the Federal style was very rarely worn on any Confederate headgear.

The cocked hat was illustrated and described in the 1861 regulations[46] and it seems that only one has survived: it has the South Carolina Palmetto tree on a black silk cockade with South Carolina button affixed – an extremely rare hat. The zouave fez, a simple wool skullcap with tassel, was worn by a small number of Confederate soldiers, possibly several battalions or regiments, but was replaced early on by more practical headgear.

Officers of the small Confederate Navy wore a visor cap very similar in pattern to the existing cap in the Federal Navy. It was supposedly gray and had a similar system of rank insignia on the front of the cap that incorporated a fouled anchor. The few contemporary photographs and surviving examples indicate that Confederate officers exercised the same broad interpretation of regulations as sailors in blue.

Confederate coats

There were three basic styles of coats worn in Confederate service but, unlike in the Federal Army, the sack coat was the least common. Officers and enlisted ranks wore variations of all of them. Officers' frock coats were quite similar in pattern to Federal coats but were usually double-breasted with two rows of seven brass buttons, although single-breasted coats did exist. Button placement for

general officers in groups of two or groups of three were sometimes seen. The collar, cuffs and edges were frequently found in branch of service color but often were just piped in branch color or without any indication of branch whatsoever. Collar insignia and sleeve galloons designated rank, although shoulder straps were infrequently seen, particularly early in the war. Sleeve galloons appeared in subdued and abbreviated patterns and even branch of service colors.[47] Epaulets were seldom seen on any occasion.

Materials utilized ranged from imported English broadcloth, wool jean, wool and cotton blends, homespun wool and wool kersey.

Above left: *Regulation staff officer's frock coat with buff facings and imported English-made staff officer's buttons. The single star on the collar identifies the rank as major.*

Above right: *Black waterproof raincoat devoid of any rank device worn by Major General T. J. Jackson when mortally wounded May 2, 1863.*

Distinctive tailoring styles existed in London, Charleston, Mobile and New Orleans that make these different patterns recognizable today. The color of the frock coat varied from very dark gray to a light tan butternut.

Enlisted men's frock coats were usually single-breasted with seven to nine buttons, but a few were regulation double-breasted styles. Some coats used black rather than blue to indicate infantry branch of service. Most frock coats were worn early in the war and replaced by the short jacket, obviously for expediency: they required less cloth and were therefore less expensive to manufacture, and every tailor knew how to construct one.[48]

Major quartermaster depots were established in Richmond, Athens, Atlanta and Columbus, Georgia, to furnish these short jackets and trousers. Confederates captured at Gettysburg were noted wearing overcoats and jackets of English manufacture. During the latter part of the war Peter Tait of Limerick, Ireland, supplied uniforms by the bale, delivered by his own ships.[49]

The Confederate government did issue some four-button sack coats patterned after prewar civilian garb. Most had a coarse cotton lining and wooden or brass buttons. A six-button sack coat with cloth epaulets authorized by state uniform regulations was issued by North Carolina to its troops.

The overcoat in Confederate service was basically a copy of the Pattern 1851 Federal Enlisted Overcoat, with and without cape, utilizing materials at hand. Some officers' coats were made of fine English wool, while enlisted men wore the same pattern made of homespun material.[50]

Officers and some enlisted men wore the vest much as it was worn in the Federal Army. Material usually matched the coat, and small brass buttons were used for closure.

The few surviving Confederate Navy coats are all gray wool frock coats of English manufacture, with regulation shoulder straps and sleeve braid. Period photographs also show this type coat worn with gray vest and trousers. At least one short blue jacket worn by a Confederate officer has survived, proof that not all were willing to abandon Navy custom to comply with regulations.

Above: Single-breasted frock coat with black facings and Federal officer's eagle buttons. Black facings were often indicative of infantry and any buttons available were used on Confederate uniforms. Lack of officer's collar insignia and sleeve galloons indicate that this is indeed an enlisted man's coat.

Confederate trousers

Confederate personnel used dismounted and mounted pattern trousers in the same fashion as did the Federal Army. Regulations called for branch of service colored striping on the outside seam of officers' trousers, such regulations being followed in haphazard fashion. Officers' trousers were usually of finer quality, particularly in the early years.

Non-commissioned officers were authorized worsted lace in branch of service color on outside trouser seams, but use became infrequent as the war progressed. Lining in most trousers was unbleached heavy cotton with a pocket on each side, and bone or metal buttons for fly closure.[51] In general, trousers were purchased by

Above left: General officer's frock coat with regulation collar insignia, buff facings and piping, button placement in groups of two, and sleeve galloons.

Above right: Frock coat of a lieutenant colonel of artillery in an unusual shade of blue gray with red facings indicating branch of service. Unusual gilt lace at the cuffs is non-regulation.

Above: *The utilitarian butternut shell jacket was the most common coat. This one has no facings and Louisiana state seal buttons. The frock coat with black tape trim and Louisiana buttons is an early war coat from that state. The multicolored pullover shirt was government-issue.*

an officer or issued to an enlisted man, together with a coat, and were of matching or very similar material initially. But trousers wore out in service at a faster rate than coats, so it was inevitable that eventually many Confederate soldiers appeared in mismatched coats and trousers in all the various shades of gray and butternut.

Shirts came in every imaginable material and pattern for officers and enlisted men. There were many quartermaster and state issue shirts and these were supplemented by civilian patterns brought or sent from home. British army shirts of cotton and flannel were imported from England by the bale.[52] Captured Federal shirts were another frequent source. All were a pullover style, with or without pockets, with two to four buttons at the neck, and cut very full.

Confederate footwear
Confederate footwear of all types came from the same primary sources as other uniform equipment: local manufacture, captured Federal equipment, and imported English stock. Officers usually purchased their boots or shoes. Boots were normally the Wellington or dragoon style and were worn by officers and mounted personnel in the cavalry or artillery. The Federal Pattern 1851 Jefferson bootee or brogan was copied in shops throughout the South and was the standard shoe for enlisted ranks. Quality of locally manufactured footwear varied widely and captured brogans were highly prized. Many thousands of sturdy shoes were run through the blockade from England, and they were greatly appreciated by those who obtained them.[53]

Above: *Well-worn brogans, somewhat different from standard Jefferson bootee – probably made in a southern shoe manufactory. Union brogans, acquired in various ways, and imported English bootees were highly prized by the Confederate soldier.*

Left: *Over the knee dragoon boots were favored by Confederate mounted personnel but many of them wore captured Federal Wellington boots or even brogans if that was all that was available. Officers purchased their own boots and type and quality varied, particularly toward the end of the war.*

Confederate insignia

Rank devices and insignia in Confederate service differed considerably from those in Federal service. The southern soldiers rarely wore branch of service insignia on the hat. If it did occur, it usually followed existing Federal patterns. Confederates did wear a number of state seal badges, crescents, crosses and stars indicating state origin. Examples of this type of badge were known for Georgia, Louisiana, Maryland, Mississippi and Texas. Many were used to pin up the brim of the hat but some were worn as breast pins. Regimental and other unit devices of local manufacture were made in small numbers.[54] There was no corps badge insignia comparable to that worn in the Federal Army.

Buttons on coats worn by officers' and enlisted ranks were sometimes branch indicative. A script or block letter I indicated infantry, C for Cavalry, A for artillery and E for engineers. Various eagles were indicative of general officers or staff officers. Almost every state issued state seal or state device buttons to some of its soldiers. Naval buttons bore the crossed cannon surmounted by a fouled anchor or a sailing ship. The Marine button was a block M. Most Confederate buttons were three-piece buttons made of stamped brass, gilt but sometimes silvered. Others were one- or two-piece, cast brass or pewter. Gross upon gross were imported from England through the blockade, and large numbers were also imported from France.[55]

Various devices on the collar indicated officer rank. There were also galloons on the sleeve from cuff to above the elbow in some cases, a combination of a modified Austrian collar and French sleeve rank designations. A general officer wore three stars surrounded by a wreath on each side of the collar, a colonel, three stars; lieutenant colonel, two stars; major, one star; captain, three horizontal bars; first lieutenant, two horizontal bars; and second lieutenant, one horizontal bar. The sleeve galloons of general officers were made of four strands of gilt lace, colonels

Below: *Tens of thousands of buttons were imported from England. The staff officer's button with eagle with CSA on the breast was very popular. The block A button was worn primarily by artillerymen. The button with the crossed cannon surmounted by a fouled anchor over CSN was obviously designed for the Navy.*

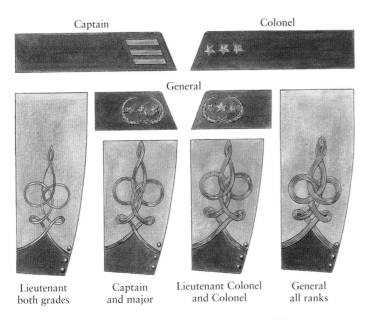

Captain

Colonel

General

Lieutenant
both grades

Captain
and major

Lieutenant Colonel
and Colonel

General
all ranks

three strands, majors and captains two strands, and lieutenants one strand. Individuality, available material and personal taste resulted in many confusing inconsistencies and variations in this system. As casualties mounted, many officers adopted less conspicuous dress. Officers' hat cords were infrequently seen and silk sword belt sashes saw limited field use. Enlisted rank was designated in the same manner as in the Federal service, with inverted vee chevrons for non-commissioned officers in branch of service color.

Naval hat insignia followed that proscribed by the 1861 Regulations and was a fouled anchor within a wreath, with rank indicated by stars above the anchor. Shoulder straps with rank devices affixed and sleeve lace were also rank and specialty indicative.

Confederate uniforms exhibited remarkable ingenuity and adaptability. The English-made uniforms were comparable to or even finer than many ranking Federal officers' uniforms. The Confederate soldier, despite his often-heterogeneous attire, affected a dashing appearance that the uniformly clad Federal soldier never quite achieved.

Small Arms and Edged Weapons

*". . . be careful to observe when the men fire, that the barrel be so directed
that the line of fire and the line of sight be in the same vertical plane."*
(Brigadier General Silas Casey, *Infantry Tactics*)

T HE WEAPON THAT ALMOST all soldiers in the conflict had to master
was, of course, the shoulder arm. A hint of what such weapons
could do was given in the war with Mexico several years before,
when the Model 1841 United States Rifle was used with deadly effect
by a Mississippi regiment commanded by then Colonel Jefferson
Davis. Dubbed thereafter the Mississippi Rifle, it was the first
officially designed and issued military percussion rifle in America,
and fathered a succession of refined models that appeared prior to
and during the Civil War itself.

Yet when war broke out in 1861, and the men mustered from
Maine to Texas, they brought with them not only the Model 1841s
left over from the Mexican War, but also a bewildering variety of
other weapons, some dating from even earlier conflicts. As state and
national governments struggled to equip their regiments, double-
barreled shotguns, hunting rifles and fowling pieces, flintlocks,
caplocks, muzzleloaders and new breechloaders, single-shot and
repeaters, pop-guns barely big enough to kill a squirrel, and
mammoth .69 and .75 caliber "smoke poles," all came into the

Below: *Model 1841 Rifles in .54
caliber and those modified and
upgraded to .58 caliber after 1855
were stored in various arsenals
around the country and many of
these weapons were seized at the
beginning of the war. This rifle was
copied by many southern
manufacturers that tried to furnish
arms for the Confederacy.*

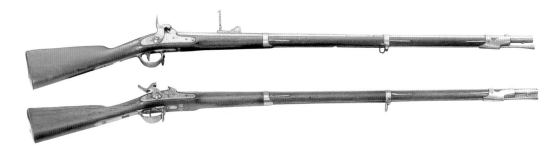

camps in the hands of the new recruits.

It has been said that no army, with the exception of the Confederate forces, ever went to war with such a variety of firearms as the Federal volunteer in the Civil War. This statement rings so true because the mid-19th century was a period of dramatic development of numerous firearms and firearms systems. The conflict became a catalyst that accelerated half a century of firearms evolution.[1]

Two generations before the Civil War, slow flintlock firing mechanisms and smoothbore musket barrels insured that a soldier could get off only one shot every couple of minutes, and that, when he did, the bullet would not go far, nor would it be likely to hit its target. The development of the percussion system, in which a copper cap could be quickly placed over a nipple at the breech, sending a spark into the powder charge when struck by the hammer, meant that three or more shots per minute could be fired. Moreover, the use of rifling grooves inside the barrel, imparting gyroscopic "spin" to the bullet as it exited, increased both the range and accuracy of the projectile, especially once the French Minie bullet was introduced. Its hollow base expanded upon firing, gripping the rifling effectively, while its cylindroconoidal shape kept it steady in flight.

Until the beginning of the Civil War the ordnance needs of the country were supplied by two national armories at Springfield, Massachusetts, and Harpers Ferry, Virginia, and six private armories. Arms were stored in twenty-four arsenals from Maine to California. The Militia Act of 1808 authorized the annual distribution of arms on a quota basis for state militia use and, under this system, a considerable number of arms were stored in facilities located in states that would eventually leave the Union.

Top: *Almost 10,000 Model 1842 Muskets were rifled and sighted between 1856 and 1859. Almost all of these arms were issued to early volunteers in the opening months of the war. These heavy .69 caliber weapons fired a large Minie ball and stayed in service until sufficient rifle muskets could be manufactured to replace them.*

Above: *275,000 Model 1842 Muskets were manufactured at Springfield and Harpers Ferry Arsenals between 1844 and 1855. With the exception of the few that were rifled and sighted all others were .69 caliber smoothbore. A large percentage of the first volunteers were armed with these obsolete weapons and some southern soldiers carried them throughout the war.*

The Ordnance Department determined in 1848 that there were about 325,000 flintlock muskets in various repositories suitable for alteration to the new percussion system of ignition.[2] The vast majority of these were the Model 1816 Muskets but some 26,000 were Model 1840 Flintlock Muskets. During the decade prior to hostilities 95 percent of these obsolete arms in storage were percussioned and some were rifled and sighted.

The Model 1842 Percussion Musket, caliber .69, superseded all flintlock arms in 1844. At the outset of hostilities there were an estimated 167,000 of these more current arms in storage in various armories. Some of these weapons also had been rifled and sighted.[3]

Rifle muskets

Secretary of War Jefferson Davis authorized the adoption of a reduced-bore, rifled firearm on July 5, 1855. This weapon was the Model 1855 Rifle Musket, caliber .58, the first rifle musket produced in the United States. It was shorter and lighter than previous muskets, with a 40-inch barrel and an effective range of 300 yards, although it was deadly to 800 yards.[4] This arm was developed at Harpers Ferry and also manufactured at Springfield. Nearly 60,000 were fabricated before the war but had already been superseded by the advent of the Model 1861 Rifle Musket.[5]

The Ordnance Department noted that there were over 525,000 muskets stored at various armories on January 21, 1861. Some 115,000 were located in those states soon to secede.[6] Certainly, a large number of Model 1842 Muskets were also in storage in southern locations.

When war broke out in April 1861 southern state forces seized all Federal installations within their respective borders, including the national armory at Harpers Ferry. The Union lost almost half its small arms manufacturing capability overnight.[7] There is every indication that at the outset of the war the Confederate soldier was as well armed as his Federal adversary.[8]

The Model 1861 Rifle Musket was the most common of all Civil War longarms, manufactured at Springfield Armory and by more than twenty contractors in the Northeast. Deliveries began in mid-

1861 and almost 1,000,000 were fabricated during the war, some 265,129 being manufactured at Springfield. This arm eliminated the troublesome Maynard tape priming device of the Model 1855 and became the standard weapon of the Civil War soldier.[9]

Soldiers armed with the Springfield loved it. It was 55.75 inches long, weighed 8.88 pounds, and was bored for a .58 caliber Minie bullet. It was simple, hardy, and could be fired three times a minute or more. With a full charge of black powder it could be deadly at 300 yards or further, and with a lucky shot could still down a man at a range of half a mile. It was lighter than many of the imported rifles first issued to regiments, was more accurate, and did not "kick" as much when fired. In the end, more Springfields, in several variants including copies, were made than any other percussion rifle ever used in America.

A Special Model 1861 Rifle Musket was introduced, and over 156,000 of this type were made, many of them by the Colt Patent Firearms Company. A considerable number were held in reserve and saw little field use. Over half a million Model 1863, Type I and Type

Above: *The .58 caliber Model 1861 Rifle Musket was the standard shoulder arm of the war, and the most often encountered in both armies. It was the ultimate development of the muzzleloading rifle musket.*

Below: *Thousands of Model 1816 Flintlock Muskets (top) were altered to percussion to extend their service life. The leather cartridge box held 40 rounds of ammunition for such a weapon. The reduced-bore .58 caliber Model 1855 Rifle Musket (bottom) was supposed to replace all the obsolete .69 caliber shoulder arms but the war interrupted those plans.*

Above: *Entrepreneurs such as Philip S. Justice furnished re-worked, poor quality weapons made of rejected or substandard parts to government purchasing agents. These weapons filled a critical need at the time and were some of the earliest deliveries of long arms. The troops to whom they were issued did not like them.*

Below: *The Sharps Rifle was probably the most popular breechloading weapon of the conflict. It was only a single-shot arm but it was simple, effective and not prone to malfunction. Both the Army and Navy purchased significant numbers of these rifles in several configurations during the war.*

II Rifle Muskets were manufactured but most were received too late to see much field service. It was the zenith of its type, and the last percussion muzzleloader accepted by Washington before the adoption of breechloaders.[10]

Rifles

Short rifles were usually issued only to the flank companies of regiments and were to be used by skirmishers. With the general acceptance of rifled longarms whole infantry regiments were thus armed. The most popular rifle was the Model 1841, originally .54 caliber. It was manufactured at Harpers Ferry from 1846 until 1855. Over 25,000 were manufactured there, while 45,500 were made under contract by E. Remington of Herkimer, New York, Robbins, Kendall and Lawrence and later Robbins and Lawrence, of Windsor, Vermont, and Tryon of Philadelphia. Many were altered and modified between 1855 and 1860 by re-rifling to .58 caliber, the addition of a long range rear sight, bayonet adapter or bayonet lug, and new steel ramrods for conical bullets.[11] It was considered the most handsome of all U.S. percussion rifles.

The Model 1855 Rifle was made in limited quantities, with only 7,317 fabricated at Harpers Ferry. It had the distinction of being the last muzzleloading rifle manufactured at a national armory, and Virginia forces captured many of the late rifles in storage at the arsenal when they seized it at the beginning of the war.

Other American made rifles were purchased and used in limited quantities by the U.S. Navy. They had obtained 1,000 Jenks

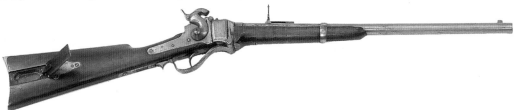

breechloading percussion rifles before the war. This arm had an unusual, and unpopular, mule ear or side hammer, the only weapon of this type purchased. In addition, 10,000 Model 1861 Plymouth Rifles, caliber .69, with special Bowie bayonets, the brainchild of Admiral Dahlgren, were purchased for use on board ship.[12] Also acquired were 500 Model 1861 Sharps and Hankins rifles, caliber .52 rimfire, with saber bayonets. Both Sharps and Spencer rifles were also used in limited quantities. All these weapons were different caliber and fired special ammunition unique to the particular arm.

Observers often wondered just who stood to suffer the greater damage from the wide variety of weapons carried onto the battlefield. At one practice shoot with .69 caliber muskets, only three out of 160 balls hit a barrel at 180 yards. General U. S. Grant later declared that a soldier armed with one of these antique "pumpkin slingers" might "fire at you all day without you ever finding out."

The firing routine

Despite their variety, almost all of the muzzleloading weapons required precisely the same routine from the soldier, a routine which Brigadier General Silas Casey in his *Infantry Tactics* (published in 1862 and which superseded Hardee's *Tactics*) reduced to a dozen commands and twenty specific motions. At the command, "Load," the soldier stood his rifle upright between his feet, the muzzle in his left hand and held eight inches from his body, at the same time moving the right hand to his cartridge box on his belt. At "Handle Cartridge," the paper-wrapped powder and bullet were brought from the box and the powder end placed between the teeth. The next two commands brought the cartridge to the muzzle, poured the powder into it, and seated the Minie in the bore. "Draw Rammer"

Below: Soldiers drilled daily in the manual of arms, use of the bayonet and loading and firing their weapons. The importance of drill could not be over-emphasized. Soldiers had to master the loading and firing sequence so that they could do it automatically in the chaos of battle without thinking or hesitation. Constant repetition made these movements become almost second nature to the soldier.

elicited the appropriate action, and "Ram" sent the bullet driving down the bore to sit on the powder charge. Another command replaced the rammer, then came "Prime." The soldier brought the weapon up and extending outward from his body with his left hand, while with his right he pulled back the hammer to the half-cock position and reached into his cap pouch, removed a cap, and placed it on the nipple.

Now came the real business. At "Shoulder" he put the rifle to his right shoulder. At "Ready" he took the proper foot stance and returned the piece to a vertical position at his right side, his right hand on the lock, his thumb pulling the hammer back to full-cock. At "Aim" up went the rifle to his right shoulder, his head to the butt so that his eye could sight between the opened "V" notch at the rear and over the blade sight at the muzzle. His finger sat ready on the trigger. The next command was "Fire," and he did.

All Civil War soldiers tended to fire high and waste inordinate amounts of ammunition. Years after the war it was calculated that, on average, a Civil War soldier on either side burned 240 pounds of powder and hurled 900 pounds of lead bullets for every single man actually hit.

By the time the first enemy bullets started to whistle over their heads the tension was so great for both officers and men that the actual start of combat came almost as a relief. The battlefield quickly became a confusion. The thick, white smoke from the black powder weapons tended to hang low, like a fog over the ground. The more guns that fired, the sooner much of the field was obscured to vision unless the wind was brisk enough to blow it away. The electric booming of the cannon and the flat, low crackling of thousands of rifles made orders nearly impossible to hear. In time, men and officers often could neither hear nor see one another, and maintaining control of even a company – much less a regiment or a brigade – could be more a matter of chance than design.

A common problem among men of both sides came with their second shot. Amid the shouting and firing, most men were not conscious of the sound of their own rifle firing, nor of the kick against their shoulders when they did. Consequently, thousands improperly reloaded their weapons – forgetting to bite off the end of the paper cartridge before ramming it home, or else neglecting to place a percussion cap on the firing nipple – but when they pulled the trigger they did not notice that their gun had failed to discharge.

Occasionally, this oversight led to a situation in which the rifle could be more dangerous to friend than foe. After the three-day Battle of Gettysburg in July 1863, the victorious Federals retrieved 27,500 rifles from the battlelines, most if not all of them dropped by the wounded and the killed. Nearly half of them were found to hold two unfired rounds in their barrels. Between three and ten loads crammed the breeches of another 6,000, and one rifle was filled almost to the muzzle with twenty-three cartridges.

Repeating rifles

By far the most technologically advanced arms were the Henry and Spencer rifles. Both were tube magazine-fed and lever-operated arms that fired self-contained waterproof rimfire cartridges, the former caliber .44 rimfire, the latter caliber .52 rimfire. The Ordnance Department bought 1,730 Henry rifles but only 1,100 were delivered before hostilities ceased. States, regiments and individuals purchased additional arms at their own expense because of advanced design and firepower.[13] The Army and Navy purchased over 12,000 Spencers and, while neither these nor the Henrys changed the course of history, both foretold the firepower of weapons of the future

The Greene Rifle was another effort to produce an advanced weapons system that went astray. Invented by Lieutenant Colonel J. Durrell Greene before the war, it was the first and only bolt action, breechloading, underhammer, oval-bore percussion arm used by the

Below: *The Spencer Rifle was one of the most advanced weapons developed during the war. The tube magazine in the butt made it a rapid-fire weapon and the self-contained metallic cartridge made it almost impervious to weather conditions. Recalcitrant ordnance personnel were slow to see the potential of the firearm.*

Bottom: *The Henry Rifle, a lever action, magazine-fed repeating arm, was the most advanced design of the period. The weapon was used in limited numbers during the conflict but its advantages were readily seen. After the war the Henry evolved into the long line of Winchester rifles, some of which are still made today.*

Federal government. During the war the Ordnance Department purchased 900 and some were used in the Battle of Antietam in 1862.[14] It is thought about 4,000 were made and some may have been purchased by state troops.

Cavalry carbines

All cavalry carbines that saw extensive service during the war were breechloading arms using a special cartridge unique to that arm. Regrettably, the government adopted no fewer than seventeen different patent breech models,[15] all firing non-interchangeable ammunition; thus, a tactical advantage became an ordnance supply nightmare. Furthermore, even companies within regiments were often armed with carbines of different make, requiring specific ammunition. Standardization was never achieved during the war but the effect of overwhelming fire superiority was not lost on those who would fight later wars.

The Spencer carbine was a magazine-fed and lever-actuated breechloader of great ingenuity. The first carbines were delivered in October 1863. Total government procurement was 51,185 by June 1, 1865, with much of Federal cavalry armed with them by the end of the war.[16] The Sharps carbine used a special linen cartridge and was the most famous single-shot carbine of the conflict. The Ordnance

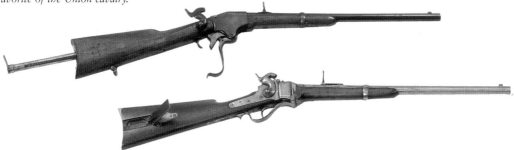

Department purchased 77,259 New Model 1859 and Model 1863 carbines during the war and had few negative reports.[17]

The Burnside carbine, 2nd, 3rd and 4th Models, used a peculiar .54 caliber metallic cartridge shaped like an ice cream cone. Invented by Ambrose E. Burnside, later a Major General in the Union Army, this carbine was the first metallic cartridge carbine accepted by the government. The Ordnance Department purchased 53,031 of them and they were extensively used, and criticized by some to whom they were issued.[18]

Above: The Smith breechloading carbine was another of the interesting patent breech arms spawned by advances in ordnance technology. The carbine at first used a rubber cartridge that was replaced by a more durable foil round. The Smith cartridge, like those of all the other patent breech carbines, was not interchangeable with any other weapon.

Two regiments of Buford's cavalry were armed with Smith carbines during the first day of the Battle of Gettysburg, July 1863. The Smith used a .50 caliber rubber cartridge later replaced by a foil round. The large spring at the breech was known to break in use. The government purchased 31,002,[19] as well as 17,728 Gallagher percussion carbines, whose major drawback was the lack of an extractor to remove the fired cartridge.[20]

In addition to these five types lesser quantities of Ballard, Gibbs, Gwyn and Campbell, Hall, Joslyn, Lindner, Maynard, Merrill, Remington, Sharps and Hankins, Starr and Wesson carbines were purchased.

Handguns

Government-purchased handguns for officers of all branches, cavalry troops and mounted artillery personnel numbered just under 400,000 during the war. The most popular calibers were .36 and .44.[21] In addition to the total purchased officially there were many handguns purchased privately by officers and enlisted men. However, the infantryman, after a twenty-mile forced march, quickly realized he didn't need the extra encumbrance of a handgun, no matter how small, and generally such weapons were promptly sold, sent home or discarded.

The leading manufacturer of handguns at the beginning of the war was the Colt Patent Firearms Company of Hartford, Connecticut. Samuel Colt had carefully developed contacts within the ordnance procurement bureaucracy to insure predominance of his products. Ordnance Department and open market purchases of the Colt Model 1860 Army Revolver amounted to more than 129,000 pieces.[22] It has been estimated that 80percent of Federal cavalrymen were armed with this sidearm at some point during service. Some 35,000 Colt Model 1851 Navy Revolvers were bought by the government[23] and there were certainly other open market and private purchases.

The Colts were simplicity itself. They were "single action," meaning that drawing back the hammer turned the cylinder from one chamber to the next after firing. Pulling the trigger was a separate action. A few "double action" revolvers, wherein pulling hard on the trigger did everything, were used, but they did not gain favor. All military-issue Colts were six-shooters, while a few five-shot Colt pocket or belt revolvers may have been carried as self-purchase weapons. A nipple sat at the back of each chamber, requiring a percussion cap. A ramming lever under the barrel pressed home each load, most often a paper "cartridge" containing ball and powder charge. The revolver could be fired as fast as one could cock the hammer and pull the trigger.

Then, of course, it was a somewhat time-consuming process to reload the cylinder. Black powder being a messy business at best when fired, a build-up of grimy fouling could slow or even stop a revolver's functioning until the arm was thoroughly cleaned. Some reports suggest that a few troopers carried fully loaded spare cylinders with them. Under these circumstances, apparently, after firing all the loads in one cylinder, it was a simple and quick process to remove the bolt holding the barrel to the frame, slide off the empty cylinder, slide a new one on, and replace the barrel. It could be done in thirty seconds, it is said, and the revolver was ready for action again. However, my own view is that the idea of disassembling a weapon under fire, on the move, particularly on horseback, is

Top: The Colt Model 1851 Navy Revolver, .36 caliber, was one of the most popular Colt products. Numbers were bought by both the Army and Navy and Confederate forces captured quantities and used them throughout the war. The major weakness was the open top frame but the single action revolver was easy to fire and simple to maintain.

Above: *The Colt Model 1860 Army Revolver, .44 caliber, saw service with all branches of service in every theater of the war. This handgun was reliable and well accepted by all who carried it. The larger caliber made it somewhat more effective as a weapon than the .36 caliber Navy but it too had the drawback of an open frame.*

fantasy. It would have been much easier to carry two revolvers, including one scavenged from dead or wounded.

In terms of numerical supply of handguns, second to Colt was E. Remington and Sons of Ilion, New York. This company furnished Beals-Remington, Old Model and New Model Revolvers in .36 and .44 caliber. It is estimated the government purchased about 127,800 Remington handguns of all models, primarily after stopping orders with Colt in November 1863 because Remington products and others were less expensive.[24] These solid frame revolvers were rugged and reliable.

The Starr Arms Company of Yonkers, New York, was the third largest supplier, with double action models in both calibers and a single action in .44 caliber. Total sales to the government were about 48,000 revolvers. The Model 1858 double action revolver was delicate and prone to malfunction in the field. The Model 1863 single action was simpler and more efficient but still generally disliked.[25]

The Ordnance Department acquired nearly 17,500 Whitney Navy Revolvers. Over 11,000 were issued to Western units, with 6,276 used by the Federal Navy.[26] Despite their fragile nature and ungainly appearance, some 11,384 Savage Revolvers were purchased by the Army, and the Navy bought an additional 1,126. Many were issued to Western cavalry units, particularly Missouri regiments.

These five makers supplied almost 380,000 revolvers of the nearly 400,000 purchased during the war. Other handguns such as the Adams, Allen and Wheelock, Butterfield, Freeman, Joslyn, Manhattan, Pettengill, Prescott and Smith and Wesson No. 2 Army Revolvers saw limited use.

There were over 10,000 obsolete Model 1842 caliber .54 single-

Above left: *Remington deprived Colt of its government contract by supplying a better and less expensive product. This New Model Navy Revolver has a tinned finish for protection during service at sea.*

Above: *The Remington New Model Army Revolver, .44 caliber, was a larger version of the Navy and employed the same strong solid frame design. Almost all of the production was for government orders.*

Above: *The self-cocking Starr Revolver in both .36 and .44 calibers was fragile and malfunctioned in field service. Only 3,000 Navy caliber revolvers were manufactured, the government purchasing 2,250. These revolvers were unpopular with the troops.*

shot pistols in the hands of state militias in 1860 and more in scattered government storage. An unknown number of Model 1836 pistols, some still in flint but most altered to percussion, were also in storage.[27] Some saw limited use in the early months of the war. Almost any handgun of the period might have been carried off to war by an enthusiastic volunteer, but on the battlefield the majority of handguns were unquestionably Colt and Remington revolvers.

Top left: *The complicated Savage-North Navy revolver had the unusual feature of the cylinder moving forward against the rear of the barrel to form a gas check during the cycle of cocking by the lower ring trigger.*

Top right: *The single action Starr was produced in mid-war because of chronic dissatisfaction with the Model 1858. It was prone to malfunction too and was just as unpopular as its predecessor.*

Above: *The government bought almost all Whitney Navy Revolvers. Army units used the majority of them but the Navy did use some 6,000.*

Edged weapons

In 1861, when the 6th Pennsylvania Cavalry was enlisted under its colonel, Richard Rush, the troopers were equipped with standard cavalry sabers, pistols, and nine-foot-long Norway fir lances with triangular edged iron spikes at the tips. A few other mounted regiments also carried lances, and a variety of pikes were issued to Confederate units, chiefly because they could not obtain better weapons. But every unit that could, soon abandoned such medieval trappings for weapons more in keeping with the war at hand.

Rush's Lancers were only an extreme example of the backward-looking logic that dominated military thinking on both sides early in the war. Few high officials in Washington or Richmond fully appreciated the fact that the invention of the percussion lock, rifling in gun barrels, and the conical Minie bullet, made virtually all previous forms of weapons obsolete. This was particularly true of edged weapons, which were effective only in a hand to hand melee, whereas any firearm bullet could wound or kill at a considerable distance. Unfortunately, it remained for soldiers in blue and gray to discover this for themselves, and to pay for the revelation with their blood.

Federal officers and non-commissioned officers of all branches and mounted troops were authorized to carry edged weapons of some type. The most common enlisted men's edged weapons were the Model 1840 and Model 1860 Cavalry Saber, the Model 1840 Light Artillery Saber, Model 1832 Foot Artillery Sword, Model 1860 Naval Cutlass, Model 1840 NCO Sword and Model 1840 Musician's Sword. These weapons were brass-mounted, plain and functional. The great majority of edged weapons in use were based upon French patterns then in vogue in Europe. The basic design differed very little. Almost all blades were relatively sharp on the cutting edge, flat or rounded on the back, with so called "blood grooves" or fullers running most of the length of both sides of the blade. Only cavalry sabers had "three bar" guards. Mounted artillery, NCO and musicians' swords had D guards. Naval cutlasses had a cup guard and foot artillery had a cross guard. The Ames Manufacturing Company, C. Roby and Company, Emerson and Silver and Sheble and Fisher fabricated most of these swords under contract to the Ordnance Department.[28]

Officers' edged weapons were more ornate and had become primarily a badge of rank by the mid-19th century. The Model 1850 Foot Officers' Sword was carried by company grade officers, lieutenants and captains, the Model 1850 Staff and Field Officers' Sword was authorized for field grade officers, majors, lieutenant colonels, colonels and general officers. The Model 1860 Staff and Field Officers' Sword, much lighter, was also authorized and saw some service. Cavalry and artillery officers' sabers were the same pattern as carried by enlisted personnel, but more elaborate and of higher quality. Naval officers generally carried the Model 1852 Naval Officers' Sword, although earlier models were in limited use.

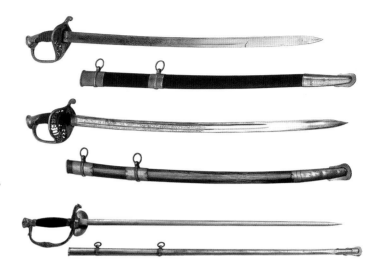

Right: *All Company grade officers were authorized Model 1850 Foot Officers' Swords. By 1861 they were little more than badges of rank with an unsharpened blade, almost useless as a weapon.*

Center: *Field grade officers were entitled to carry the Model 1850 Staff and Field Officer's Sword. It was very similar to the foot officers' sword but had the letters US in the decorative guard.*

Right: *The Model 1860 Staff and Field Officer's Sword was supposed to replace the earlier model. Its only favorable attribute was that it was very light; it was absolutely useless as a weapon. Serving officers did not favor it.*

There were a considerable number of non-regulation officers' swords and sabers imported from Solingen, Germany, the blade capital of Europe, and a lesser number from England and France. Most generally followed authorized patterns but some were quite elaborate and unusual.[29]

Soldiers, regardless of rank or branch of service, quickly learned that no sword or saber was a match for a six-shot revolver, breech-loading carbine, or rifle musket. While some officers used them to rally and encourage their soldiers, many others placed them in baggage trains. Enlisted men seemed to lose an inordinate number, even though they were charged for them.

Right: *Pattern 1851 Sword Belt with hangers and cast brass rectangular eagle sword belt plate. The belt is of finer grade finished leather with embossed line decoration along both edges. The hangers attach to the two ring mounts on the sword scabbard when the sword is carried.*

The standard sword belt for officers during the Civil War was the Pattern 1851, with a rectangular brass sword belt plate. Individual officers privately purchased almost all sword belts and there was a wide range of quality. Sword belts were available from military regalia retailers such as Ball, Black & Co., Schuyler, Hartley & Graham, and Tiffany & Co. in New York City; Bailey & Co., Evans and Hassall, and W. H. Horstmann & Sons in Philadelphia, and M. W. Galt & Brothers and Hunt and Goodwin in Washington, D.C.

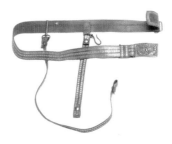

The sword belt for general officers was made of Russian leather with three stripes of gold embroidery. Sword belts for all other officers were black leather, often embossed with lines along both edges or completely covered with embossed designs. Some were piped in branch of service color. The belt plate was rectangular in shape, made of cast brass with a gilt finish, depicting the arms of the United States, an eagle, shield and scroll with the motto "E PLUIBUS UNUM" ("Out of many, one" – referring to thirteen colonies united into one nation) within a silver wreath.[30] A small number have been noted with a fine chased finish suggesting jeweler craftsmanship. Variations with state seals or letters exist. All had sword or saber hangers for attachment of the edged weapon and many had over-the-shoulder straps for support.

The 1851 Regulation black buff or black bridle leather waist belt with 1839 Pattern oval brass U.S. belt plate was the standard waist belt of the Federal soldier. This oval brass plate was 2$\frac{1}{2}$ x 3$\frac{1}{2}$ inches and attached by oval studs to the belt until it was superseded by plates with arrowhead hooks. This belt supported the cap box and bayonet scabbard, and sometimes the cartridge box. The same belt, fitted with a rectangular eagle plate, was designated for non-commissioned officers.[31] Earlier white buff belts with the same plate were used infrequently early in the war. Some state troops wore a distinctive plate rather than the oval U.S. plate. Oval plates with SNY (State of New York) and OVM (Ohio Volunteer Militia) were issued in some quantity. A smaller VMM (Volunteer Militia

Left: Pattern 1851 General Officer's Sword Belt with hangers and high quality sword belt plate. The belt is embossed with three rows of gilt and the hangers two in this specimen. Most have three rows of gold bullion thread sewn to the belt.

Below left: Enlisted man's dyed brown buff leather waist belt with oval brass Pattern 1839 US belt plate. Belts such as this were worn by foot soldiers throughout the Army. Like other pieces of field gear it was simple and functional.

Below: Pattern 1851 dyed brown buff saber belt with hangers, over the shoulder support strap and rectangular brass eagle plate. This belt also supported a revolver with holster, cap box and pistol ammunition box. The over the shoulder strap helped balance the load.

Below: *The cap box was worn on the right side of the waist belt and contained copper percussion caps. The percussion cap looked like a small top hat.*

Below: *Cartridge box and shoulder belt with eagle breast plate for .58 caliber ammunition. The box has a wallet on the front for gun tools and inner flap to protect cartridges from bad weather.*

Maine) was issued to early units of that state, and oval plates bearing the great seals of the states of Maryland and Pennsylvania were also issued in limited quantities.

The same regulations called for cavalry waist belts of buff or bridle leather with rectangular sword belt plate of the same pattern worn by officers but of lesser quality, and with hangers and over-the-shoulder strap. The same basic belt without shoulder strap was proscribed for mounted light artillery personnel. Black buff or bridle leather waist belts with integral frog for the Model 1832 foot artillery short sword using the Pattern 1851 rectangular eagle plate were issued to foot artillery units.[32]

Federal accouterments

The cap box and cartridge box were primary components of the set of accouterments worn by soldiers to carry ammunition for their firearms. In both armies the standard pre-battle issue of ammunition amounted to sixty rounds of cartridges and percussion caps. The soldier put the caps in the leather cap-box on his belt. Forty rounds were carried in double-tiered tins within the cartridge box and the additional twenty rounds, two packs, were carried in the haversack.

In the North, cartridge and cap boxes were supplied by the Ordnance Department and fabricated at several government arsenals and by many civilian contractors. In practice, complete sets of accouterments – including cap and cartridge boxes, waist and shoulder belts with plates and bayonet scabbards – were delivered. Between January 1861 and June 1865 more than 2,000,000 sets of such infantry accouterments were purchased.[33]

Cap boxes evolved through a series of improvements. Two basic types were manufactured during the war. One had the latch tab integral to the flap and the other had it sewn to the flap. The belt straps of earlier cap boxes were sewn only, while later cap boxes had the straps reinforced with copper rivets. Initially, most were fabricated at government arsenals.

Cartridge boxes included several patterns due to the diverse nature of ammunition required by various arms in use. The primary difference was size, dictated by the ammunition carried, which would

Below: *Bridle leather carbine cartridge box with two belt loops on the reverse. This box has an accessory wallet and wooden block insert bored to accommodate metallic or prepared cartridges.*

Above: *Bridle leather pistol cartridge box with two belt loops on the reverse. There is no inner flap or accessory wallet. The box holds two packs of six revolver cartridges, either .36 or .44 caliber.*

have been .54, .58 or .69 caliber. Boxes most often encountered were the patterns of 1857, 1861, March 1864 and July 1864, although older patterns were issued early in the war. The July 1864 pattern dispensed with the oval brass US box plate that had been affixed to the cartridge box for over twenty years and substituted an embossed U.S. on the leather flap.[34]

The other integral component of the accouterment set was the bayonet and scabbard. Almost all muskets and rifle muskets were fitted with a triangular socket bayonet, and most rifles were designed to accept a saber bayonet. When not attached to the firearm the bayonet was carried in a leather scabbard mounted on the waist belt.

Cavalry carbine cartridge boxes were usually smaller with less capacity than rifle, rifle musket and musket boxes, and had wood or tin inserts to accommodate the different metallic and paper cartridges used with the various carbines in service. Special boxes existed for the Spencer, Sharps and some other carbines, but most used a multi-purpose box.[35]

Revolver holsters were an integral part of accouterments for officers and mounted personnel. Because of the various model handguns in service the holsters had to be made to fit the arm. All were black bridle leather with full flap and latch tab to cover the weapons. A reinforced loop on the reverse allowed the holster to be

Above: *.58 caliber rifle musket cartridge box with brass oval US box plate affixed and brown buff leather shoulder belt with eagle breast plate. This was a standard size cartridge box for infantry that held forty rounds. Thousands of sets of accouterments were fabricated by a large number of private contractors and several government arsenals. Surplus accouterments were sold to the general public for years after the war until the early 1960s.*

carried on the sword, saber or waist belt. A special cartridge box was used to carry revolver ammunition and was found in at least two sizes depending on caliber of ammunition.

Gun wrenches were a necessary tool for the care and maintenance of firearms and many weapons, particularly various carbines, required special tools for this task. Regardless of weapon, most tools were combinations of screwdriver/nipple wrench of some form. These tools were often carried in an accessory pocket within the cartridge box.

Haversacks, knapsacks, and canteens

The Pattern 1851 black-painted canvas haversack with liner was a standard issue item to all soldiers. It was used primarily to carry food rations and necessary items not stored in the knapsack. The cotton inner sack was ineffectually utilized to prevent grease from soiling the uniform. Millions were fabricated during the war and most became worn out in service. Officers' haversacks were usually private purchase, multi-compartmented leather bags, often of hand-tooled fine leather.

The knapsack was another issue item to all foot soldiers and was worn on the back with leather carrying straps over each shoulder. All spare clothing, extra shoes, mess equipment, personal items, wool blanket, gum blanket and shelter half were supposedly carried in it. The Model 1855 Knapsack, a soft double bag, painted canvas piece, was the most common type. The material used was similar to that used in the haversack. It replaced the rigid frame box-type pre-war knapsack that still continued in use for some time. There were a number of non-regulation or patent knapsacks in use in limited numbers throughout the war.[36]

Yet another important piece of personal equipment was the canteen. The Model 1858 canteen with cloth cover and cotton sling was standard issue. A similar canteen with concentric rings for added strength was furnished after 1861.[37] The $7\frac{1}{2}$ inch diameter body of the canteen was covered in blue, gray or brown wool or cotton stitched around the edges. Private purchase canteens with filters or other patent devices were frequently used.

The Quartermaster Department supplied wool blankets and state contractors supplied many of lesser quality. Issue blankets were normally dark brown or gray with black stripes on both ends and an embroidered US in the center.[38] A considerable number of non-regulation blankets were procured from various sources.

Naval personnel were issued appropriate black leather accouterments that were often embossed with USN or the Navy Yard where issued. The cartridge and cap box were standard configuration. The boarding axe and scabbard, skeleton revolver holster, Pattern 1862 buff leather waist belt with japanned iron buckle, and fuse pouch were unique to naval accouterments.[39]

Imported arms

There has been little focus on and scant attention paid to the tens of thousands of English and other European arms imported by both combatants, particularly in the first two years of the war. Many of these weapons were obsolete, some considered absolutely useless, but they filled a critical need in time of emergency. Others were proved to be fine arms comparable to any made in the United States.

Federal arms agents had notable success in England and Europe. Herman Boker and Company, New York, imported 188,054 Austrian, Prussian, French and Belgian arms of varying calibers from .54 to .71 between November 1861 and May 1862. Marcellus Hartley imported 110,424 Pattern 1853 British Rifle Muskets between August and December 1862. Schuyler, Hartley and Graham

Above: The rigid box knapsack with blanket roll was used early in the war by some state troops. The "bullseye" canteen was issued in 1862.

Below: The Pattern 1853 English Enfield Rifle Musket, .577 caliber (top), was imported in large numbers by both sides. The Austrian Lorenz Rifle (bottom), .54 and .58 caliber, was also imported in large numbers. It was not as well finished as the Springfield or Enfield but proved to be a reliable arm.

Above: *The Model 1854 Lefaucheux pinfire revolver, according to recent research, appears to have seen more use than previously thought. They were in the hands of Federal troops in April 1862 at the Battle of Shiloh and there evidently were a number in Confederate hands in 1864.*

Below: *Machinery captured at Harpers Ferry was installed in Richmond and produced rifle muskets, short rifles and carbines of a modified 1855 pattern without the Maynard priming mechanism through out the war. This facility was easily the most important source for small arms within the Confederacy.*

brought in 35,745 Pattern 1853 Rifle Muskets, and Naylor and Co. some 189,700.[40]

More than 600,000 Pattern 1853 Enfield Rifle Muskets, in .577 caliber, and derivative arms account for the bulk of English arms imported and sold to the Federal government. This weapon was second only in quantity to the Model 1861 Rifle Musket in the hands of the soldiers and was well liked. Some 226,000 Austrian Lorenz Rifles, Model 1854, calibers .54 and .58, were also imported.[41] Smaller quantities of contemporary and obsolete Belgian and French longarms have been noted. All purchases of foreign long arms ceased by the end of 1862, with the exception of Pattern 1853 English arms, and those stopped in July 1863.

Foreign handguns played only minor roles during the war. One of several exceptions was the French-made Model 1854 Lefaucheux pinfire revolver that used a twenty-five-year-old system involving a self-contained brass cartridge with a small pin protruding from the side at the base, acting as a percussion cap when struck by the hammer. Colonel George L Schuyler purchased 10,000 Lefaucheux revolvers in fall 1861. By the end of the war the Ordnance Department had procured a total of 11,833 M1854 pinfire revolvers. Most were sent to western troops by 1863. In quantity issued, this revolver ranked just behind Colt, Remington and Starr handguns.[42] Raphael and Perrin revolvers were purchased by the government in small numbers and saw little if any field use.

Confederate small arms

When the Civil War began, there was no active small arms industry in the South. The fledgling armed forces of the Confederacy were totally dependent upon arms seized at Federal installations within their borders, arms received under the Militia Act of 1808 and stored in the respective states, the few arms manufactured for state forces

nearly a decade earlier, and arms purchased in the North in the short months between secession and active hostilities. These sources provided an estimated 285,000 to 300,000 arms,[43] the bulk of which were percussion smoothbore muskets together with a few more modern rifles and rifle muskets – the very same type of weapons in the hands of the Federal foe already noted.

Realizing the immediate need for additional arms, Confederate authorities sent agents to Europe to scour the arms markets for any weapons that were available. The result was the importation of large quantities of arms and equipment, particularly from England and Austria, to supplement ordnance requirements while Herculean efforts were made to establish a sufficient small arms industry in the Confederacy. Most current research indicates that over 200,000 English Pattern 1853 rifle muskets and derivative arms actually reached the Confederacy. Some 100,000 Austrian Model 1854 Lorenz rifles were purchased in Vienna in 1862[44] and most made it through the blockade before the end of the war.

The English Kerr Revolver, .44 caliber, was imported, and possibly 8,500 were used by army and navy units. This revolver was a product of the London Armoury Company that had a close connection to Sinclair, Hamilton and Company,[45] one of the major suppliers of English military material to the Confederacy.

Another imported handgun, the fascinating LeMat "grapeshot" revolver, was one of the more unusual weapons of the war. A New Orleans doctor of French ancestry patented the two-barrel, ten-shot weapon in 1856. It had a cylinder that held nine .42 caliber bullets fired through an upper barrel in orthodox single action revolver fashion, and the cylinder revolved around a single smoothbore barrel of .63 caliber. The hammer had an adjustable nose to allow selective firing of the chambers in the cylinder or the lower shot barrel. A small number of these prewar revolvers were made in Philadelphia, with wartime production occurring in Belgium, then France and finally England, where they were inspected and accepted by Confederate ordnance officials.[46] Around 4,000 of these percussion revolvers in several configurations were imported during the war.

Above: *The English Kerr Revolver was made under contract by the London Armoury Company for the Confederate government. Both the Confederate army and navy purchased these fine revolvers. The number of imported Kerrs was far larger than the production of any of the local revolver manufacturers.*

Above: *The LeMat revolver is one of the more fascinating handguns of the war. Generals J. E. B. Stuart and P. G. T. Beauregard had LeMats, and Major Henry Wirz, commandant of Andersonville, had one too. Prone to breakage and often failing to pass inspection, these arms nevertheless have captured the imagination.*

Another very productive source of arms for the Confederacy was through capture and battlefield salvage after engagements through the spring of 1863. Many thousands of more modern firearms were acquired in this manner. This was frustrating in the case of various patent breech and metallic cartridge carbines. Confederate ordnance did not have the capability to manufacture the necessary ammunition for such arms and they became useless after ammunition was expended. This was particularly true of Spencer arms in the latter part of the conflict.

Regrettably, the least productive source was the ordnance complex painstakingly developed in the Confederacy. There was no existing small arms industry to speak of in the South at the beginning of the war. Arms that had been made in the pre-war years were not suited to mass production or military service. Lack of experience and technical skills required to manufacture arms was chronic and never overcome. Added to that was the frequent shortage of adequate basic materials.

The Richmond Armory was the single most productive arms facility in the Confederacy, producing arms from October 1861 through January 1865. Estimated production of new arms was nearly 38,000 weapons including rifle muskets, short rifles and carbines. Repaired and refurbished various model arms amounted to almost 50,000 pieces.[47] These figures together exceed the production of all other arms facilities in the South during the war.

Fayetteville Armory in North Carolina received the rifle machinery captured at Harpers Ferry. With this equipment set up in the seized Federal Arsenal complex some 8,600 to 8,900 excellent .58 caliber rifles were manufactured from 1862 until early 1865.[48] Without the machinery taken at Harpers Ferry neither the production in Richmond nor that in Fayetteville could have been accomplished. These two sources provided nearly 100,000 arms during the war. The

Below: The Fayetteville Rifle was made by machinery captured at Harpers Ferry and was the finest two-band rifle made in the Confederacy, comparing favorably with any arms made in the North. Unfortunately, production was always insufficient to meet the needs of the army.

Confederate war effort would have been doomed to early failure without these facilities.

Cook and Brother produced nearly 7,800 rifles, musketoons and carbines from 1861 until 1864.[49] These arms were close copies of the imported English Pattern 1853 arms. Initial production began in New Orleans but the company was forced to relocate inland to Athens, Georgia, upon Federal occupation of New Orleans in 1862. Had it not been for an opportunistic Federal sentry who allowed a schooner laden with steel and iron to pass in return for $20.00, the Cook operation would have lost much of its stock of raw material. The Cook facility was the largest private armory in the South and furnished firearms and bayonets not only for the central government but also for the state of Alabama.[50] It is worth noting that Cook had a contract to furnish 50,000 arms to the Confederacy yet managed to deliver fewer than 8,000. Such disappointments were the norm in Confederate ordnance procurement throughout the war. No amount of patriotism and good intentions could overcome inexperience and lack of skilled manpower.

There was always a shortage of carbines for Confederate mounted

Above: *Cook and Brother was the most prolific private armory in the Confederacy. The British Pattern 1853 Short Rifle and other derivative arms were the patterns for arms produced there.*

Below: *Efforts were made by S. C. Robinson and the central government in Richmond to copy the Sharps Carbine so favored by northern cavalry, with unsatisfactory results.*

Bottom: *The always pressing need for arms for mounted troops and availability of damaged rifle musket barrels resulted in the production of the Richmond Carbine.*

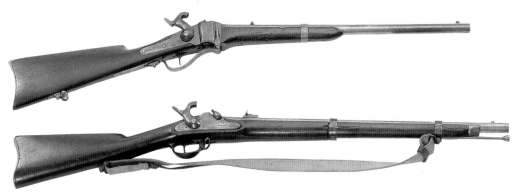

troops and it was not unusual for such units to be armed with short rifles or rifle muskets. This was not a great inconvenience since these troops typically fought dismounted anyway but every effort was made to produce adequate carbines. One of the chief sources was S. C. Robinson and Company in Richmond who endeavored to manufacture a copy of the Sharps breechloading carbine so favored by Federal troops. Reports from the field indicated that the arms were unsatisfactory, with a number bursting during use. The factory was subsequently taken over by the government and produced over 4,500 carbines before ceasing work in spring 1864. G. W. Morse developed a novel brass-framed breechloading carbine that was manufactured at the South Carolina State Military Works at Greeneville. The weapon utilized a reloadable metallic percussion cartridge. It was an advanced design with promise, but only about 1,000 were produced and most saw limited state service.

Numerous individuals and companies endeavored to provide arms for the beleaguered Confederacy and individual Southern states. North Carolina had contracts with no fewer than five different manufacturers and Alabama, Georgia and South Carolina also sought arms. This manifestation of states' rights often put state ordnance procurement in direct competition with government ordnance procurement, just as it did with importation of foreign arms, with resultant higher prices and added frustration to all concerned.

Below: Samuel Griswold manufactured a reasonably faithful copy of Samuel Colt's Navy revolver with inadequate and unskilled labor and intermittent shortages of raw material in the hamlet of Griswoldville, Georgia. These brass-framed revolvers were some of the best manufactured in the South under adverse conditions.

Bottom: The copy of the Whitney Navy revolver by Spiller and Burr, and subsequently the government, was another effort to manufacture a firearm of a proven pattern. Constant shortages of basic raw materials forced the use of substitutes at every turn – brass for iron, iron for steel.

Confederate revolvers

Southern revolver production shared all the same problems of inexperience, lack of skilled labor and raw materials. Four sources, Griswold and Gunnison, Leech and Rigdon, Rigdon, Ansley & Co. and Spiller and Burr, furnished 90percent of the handguns manufactured in the Confederacy. With the exception of the latter, all copied the Colt Model 1851 Revolver. Spiller and Burr copied the Whitney .36 caliber Navy Revolver. Griswold and Spiller revolvers substituted brass for iron in the fabrication of frames for their handguns because of iron shortages and ease of brass working for

Left: *Most Confederate cavalry sabers were copies of US Model 1840 or 1860 sabers. Materials at hand and ease of manufacture determined the result. This saber has an unstopped blade and rough-finished brass hilt. The scabbard is sheet iron with a crude brazed seam and brass mounts, with file marks still evident.*

unskilled labor. These four manufacturers delivered only about 10,000 handguns during the whole war, a fraction of those delivered by Colt and Remington and just slightly more than were imported from England.

Confederate edged weapons

Confederate edged weapons were in most cases copies of existing Federal patterns. Major manufacturers such as Boyle, Gamble and MacFee in Richmond, Louis Haiman & Brothers in Columbus, Georgia, the Confederate States Armory in Kenansville, North Carolina, and Kraft, Goldsmith & Kraft in Columbia, South Carolina, developed patterns unique to those respective firms. Of course the letters CS or CSA were included in the hilt decoration of these weapons. Production of most suppliers of Confederate edged weapons was limited, although the output of a few must have been

Left top: *This saber with a straight, noticeably wavy, unstopped blade favors somewhat the English Pattern 1853 Trooper's saber. The wooden scabbard with sheet iron mounts and brass rings is an excellent example of substitution with material at hand.*

Left center: *The Confederate naval sword made in England exhibits the highest quality of workmanship. It is one of the few Confederate swords of original design, not a copy of a U.S. pattern.*

Left bottom: *The light artillery saber by Thomas, Griswold of New Orleans is proof that the quality of some Confederate edged weapons compared favorably with U.S. products.*

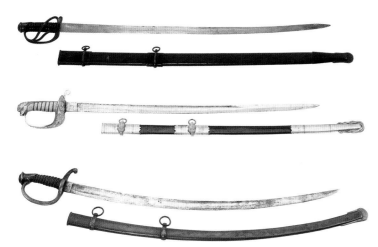

Top: *Officer's sword belt with hangers and two-piece interlocking CS belt plate. The quality of the casting of the belt plate and the quality of the leather belt with embossed borders are the indicators that this is an officers' belt. Those for enlisted personnel, though quite similar, do not exhibit the same fine finish.*

Above: *Enlisted man's waist belt with cast brass rectangular CSA belt plate. The latter was cast at the Atlanta Arsenal and is the most common of this type. Despite the great variety of Confederate plates, all were made in relatively limited quantities. The brass frame or iron roller buckle was the most common buckle.*

relatively substantial based upon surviving examples.

Officers' swords and sabers were higher quality, some with finely cast hilts and gilt finish, but oil cloth wrap substituted for leather on the grip and plain single-strand brass or even iron wire grip wrap. There were exceptions, such as the extraordinary presentation swords of Thomas, Griswold of New Orleans made early in the war.[51] These were at least as good as any blades made in the North, including those by Tiffany & Company in New York.

Enlisted men's swords and sabers were much plainer and had less decoration. Most cavalry sabers were copies of the Model 1840 or 1860 Federal saber. The scabbards of some were made of copper or even wood rather than iron and the rough finish on many was typical of unskilled labor assembly.

Thousands of edged weapons were imported from England and lesser numbers from mainland Europe. Both English infantry and cavalry models were acquired and many had Confederate or southern state motifs applied on order. The sword authorized by Confederate Naval Regulations that was manufactured in England is particularly interesting. It was one of the few Confederate edged weapons that was truly original in design and did not copy U.S. swords. The pommel and backstrap formed a sea monster and the guard bore the arms of the Confederate Navy and floral decoration in the form of cotton and tobacco leaves.[52]

There is a quaintness about many Confederate edged weapons that makes them recognizable at a glance. The blades of most are unstopped at the hilt. There is no ricasso where the blade fits into the hilt, and some blades are noticeably wavy. Those with metal scabbards have crudely soldered seams. Some of the brass hilts and mountings even seem to have a rose color.

Sword belts and belt plates

Sword belts for these Confederate weapons again paralleled those of Federal manufacture but with obvious subtle changes to reflect Confederate origin. The two-piece CS belt plate was by far the most common and came in officers' and enlisted men's quality. Some states such as Virginia, Louisiana, North Carolina and South Carolina had similar sword belt plates with the state seal adorning the disc.

There were a great variety of waist belts used by Confederate troops. The general issue brass frame buckle or plain iron roller buckle were the types of buckles most commonly used with these belts. There were a great many belt plates bearing CS and CSA, some of brass, iron or pewter, and plates bearing state seals or state designating letters of almost every Southern state were also used but in very limited numbers compared to the frame and roller types.

Confederate accouterments

Early in the war cartridge and cap boxes made by facilities such as the Baton Rouge Arsenal exhibited the same good craftsmanship as those made in the North. Lack of raw materials soon forced Southern manufacturers to develop substitutes for critical materials such as leather, and by 1863 black-painted, multiple-thickness canvas was used in the manufacture of waist belts, cartridge and cap boxes, and even the frogs for bayonet scabbards. Other ersatz substitutes used were lead and even wood for brass, so that the closure buttons on Confederate accouterments were often found made of those materials.

Thousands of bales of hides and huge numbers of sets of accouterments were also imported from England, while many thousands of captured Federal cap and cartridge boxes were also issued. Usually the Confederate soldiers threw away the US box plates but sometimes these box plates were worn inverted on the cartridge box and even the waist belt. Some states – Georgia, Mississippi and South Carolina – issued a very limited number of accouterments with state plates early in the war.

Weapon accessories

Cavalry carbine boxes were much the same as the Federal counterpart but with far fewer variations for different carbines. Again, material shortages resulted in the use of lead and wood closure buttons. Confederate revolver holsters also followed the same patterns as their Federal counterparts, primarily because most of them carried Federal

Below: Confederate carbine cartridge box, closely paralleling its Federal counterpart. The leather is slightly lesser quality and stitching is not quite as good. A lead closure button has been substituted for the brass one of the Federal box.

Above: *This CS-embossed .69 caliber cartridge box with sling is an atypical example. Most Confederate-made accouterments were devoid of any markings.*

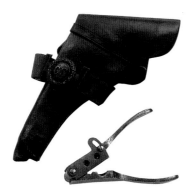

revolvers. Many Confederate holsters eliminated the flap closure button and instead the flap fitted through a leather loop for closure. Simplicity and economy were always a consideration.

Gun tools or gun wrenches were provided with weapons. In the case of infantry arms usually this was a generic dual-purpose instrument that acted as a cone wrench to change the cone in the barrel, and a screwdriver to disassemble and reassemble the weapon. Pistol tools were smaller, with the same function and usually revolver-specific.

These tools were normally carried in the accessory compartment on the front of the cartridge box, stuffed in the cap box or any convenient pocket. Thousands accompanied the English and Austrian weapons for which they were made.

Top: *Leather holster for the English Kerr Revolver on a leather waist belt with brass two-piece interlocking CS belt plate thought to have been made in Richmond. The holster flap fits through a leather keeper.*

Above: *Iron double-cavity bullet mold with sprue cutter for casting Colt .44 caliber bullets. Molds were normally cased with revolvers but were available separately.*

Bayonets

While lances appeared only briefly, and disappeared quickly, a near cousin, in concept at least, remained on the battlefields throughout the war. The bayonet appeared more than a century earlier, at a time when flintlock muskets were cumbersome, slow in firing, and woefully inaccurate. Theory called for the firing of a volley or two, creating more smoke and noise than damage, and then a spirited assault, trusting to the gleaming bayonets at the muzzles of the guns to do the real work, making the blade yet again just an extension of the infantryman's arm.

It was sound thinking given the state of shoulder arms in the 18th century. Failing to appreciate the impact of the rifle, however, commanders going into the Civil War assumed that the same tactics should apply. Literally without exception, every properly equipped infantryman on both sides, perhaps as many as two million men in

Right: *Richmond Armory three square socket bayonet, with lead- rather than brass-tipped leather scabbard. Lack of steel forced the Richmond Armory to modify bayonet manufacture to utilize wrought iron.*

all, carried bayonets of varying size and description. Their variety was almost bewildering.

The average bayonet was eighteen inches or more in length, triangular in cross section, and tapering to a sharp point, with deep grooves between its edges. Some, however, were much shorter, little more than knives, while others stretched up to two feet from the muzzle of a rifle. Some, like the saber bayonet used with Model 1853 British Short Rifles, were literally swords. The British Brunswick sword bayonet actually resembled an ancient Roman short sword more than anything else.

Yet the men never did trust their bayonets, nor, with very few exceptions, did they ever have occasion to use them as intended. Despite all the intent and orders of their commanders, most Civil War soldiers never came to actual hand-to-hand fighting, and therefore never used their bayonets in combat. Instead, they jammed them in the ground at their bivouacs or into the walls of their winter huts, finding that the socket designed to attach the bayonet to the muzzle of a gun was ideal for holding a candle. More often still, a bayonet, this time attached to the rifle, made a perfect spit for roasting some poor farmer's chicken or ham over an open campfire.

Triangular socket bayonets and brass- or iron-hilted saber bayonets were fitted to most Confederate infantry longarms. Scabbards for these bayonets were usually made of leather with brass or tin mounts and were worn on the waist belt. The great majority of bayonets were the Model 1855 that fitted all .58 caliber Model 1855, 1861, 1863 and Richmond rifle muskets and .69 caliber socket bayonets used with Model 1816 alterations and Model 1842 muskets. Richmond Armory made a copy of the Model 1855 socket bayonet and also a 3-square socket bayonet with iron blade and steel tip.[53] This bayonet had no flutes on the blade. All three surfaces were flat. Short rifles utilized a sword bayonet patterned after the U.S. Model 1855 saber bayonet, and there were many minor variations. Most were heavy and awkward and manufacture was terminated early in 1864 due to material shortage. Thousands of English Pattern

Above: Georgia Armory brass-hilted saber bayonet and scabbard with buff leather integral frog and tin mounts. Instead of a brass toe mount on the scabbard, this one has been fabricated of sheet tin, another Confederate substitute. Manufacture of saber bayonets ceased in 1864 for lack of raw materials.

Below: *Officers often carried a private purchase leather haversack of the type shown. The shaped wood canteen is one of the rare Nuckolls Patent.*

Above left: *Confederate personalized Federal Model 1858 spheroid canteen with carefully embroidered rendition of the 1st National flag on the cover.*

Above right: *Confederate artilleryman's brown leather haversack manufactured by Julius Darrow of Augusta, Georgia, almost an exact copy of its Federal counterpart.*

1853 socket bayonets and Austrian Pattern 1854 socket bayonets were imported, along with those firearms. These bayonets were not interchangeable with any other arms.

As a weapon the bayonet had more of a psychological effect than actual use in the Civil War. Their use as a digging tool in dire straits foretold the advent of the personal entrenching tool nearly fifty years later. In the end, though, there could be little more eloquent testimony to the obsolescence of edged weapons in warfare by the time of the Civil War than the fact that out of the millions of wounds inflicted between 1861 and 1865, only four-tenths of one percent – four out of every thousand – were inflicted by a sword or bayonet.

Haversacks and canteens

Haversacks were carried by all Confederate officers and men and were obtained from many sources. Some were home made, others arsenal made, a large number were captured from Federal sources, and others were state issue. Officers' haversacks, like their Federal counterparts, were usually more elaborate. Some of these were multi-compartmented leather bags but most were cotton or painted canvas affairs involving minimal skills to fabricate. Size tended to vary considerably but the average was about 12 × 12 inches.

The wooded drum canteen was one of those pieces of equipment that was synonymous with the Confederate soldier, and one of the favorite souvenirs taken home by Federal soldiers. Construction consisted of two sides with slats held by iron or brass rims. The rims had three loops around the circumference for a shoulder strap, and the top slats of the canteen were tapped with a wooden neck and stopper.[54] Another type was made of two halves of wood pegged together. In actuality, the tin drum canteen was much more prevalent, as was the captured Federal Model 1858 canteen which was used in enormous numbers as fast as they could be acquired.

Knives

Another piece of equipment considered indispensable in the early months of the war was the large D-guard knife or side knife carried off to war by so many eager volunteers. These big knives were

sometimes arsenal made, such as those fabricated by the Confederate States Armory at Kenansville, NC, and Boyle, Gamble & Co., Richmond, but more often the product of the village smithy and made from old files or wagon springs. It was not unusual to find a knife with a fourteen or sixteen inch blade. Fearsome in appearance, they were no match for a Spencer seven-shot rifle or a Colt or Remington revolver. The first hard march usually saw these heavy, cumbersome knives placed in company baggage or dropped in the nearest ditch.

Contrary to popular opinion, not all Confederate soldiers carried blanket rolls. A great many carried either the soft knapsack or the rigid box knapsack all through the war. As with all other equipment, large numbers of captured Federal soft double bag knapsacks were used and thousands of English Pattern 1854 Knapsacks were secured through the military outfitters, S. Isaac, Campbell & Co., and run through the blockade. Blankets were carried in quantity and came from varied sources. Many were state issue, some government issue, and large numbers were acquired from local sources.

Naval accouterments

Naval accouterments used aboard ships outfitted overseas were probably the English pattern then in use. Those issued for use on the river fleets were locally made, and likely copies of existing Federal types.

The Civil War was the last American war where soldiers went into combat with so many non-standard weapons and diverse and confusing uniforms. By the end of the war the effectiveness and economy of standardization of uniforms and equipment had become readily apparent to both combatants. Confederate soldiers were not the barefoot and ragged warriors sometimes portrayed. They were as well armed and well uniformed as their Federal adversary but they were numerically outnumbered.

Above: *D-guard bowie knife and scabbard made by the Confederate States Armory, Kenansville, N. C., and a side knife with bowie blade made by Boyle, Gamble, Richmond.*

Below: *Naval accouterments. The boarding axe with scabbard was used primarily as a tool for cutting away fallen rigging and clearing the area of debris rather than as a weapon for fighting. The waist belt had a japanned iron buckle to retard salt-water corrosion.*

CHAPTER THREE

Artillery

"We are required to move the guns about by hand, over the field, to front and to rear, in echelon and in line, to sponge and load and fire in mimic warfare, until our arms ache, and we long for rest."

(Private Benjamin Jones, Surry Light Artillery of Virginia)

Below: *Huge 15-inch Rodman gun mounted on a wrought iron center pintle barbette carriage in Battery Rodgers near Alexandria, Virginia, one of the defensive forts around Washington, D.C. This type of ordnance was first manufactured at Ft. Pitt in 1860.*

*B*Y THE TIME OF the Civil War there were five basic categories of weapons considered to be artillery. These were field, siege and fortification, seacoast, mountain and prairie, and volley or rapid-fire guns (the forerunners of modern machine guns.[1]) Each classification had specific qualities and intended purposes. Field guns were light, mobile pieces of relatively small caliber, flat trajectory and limited range; they could travel with the army and rapidly go into action. Siege and fortification guns were heavier, of larger caliber and could be moved only with considerable effort. The larger of this type were intended for permanent placement in fixed fortifications. This latter employment applied also to the large seacoast guns. The mountain and prairie guns were very light, of small caliber and could be carried broken down for carriage by pack mules.[2] The embryonic volley or rapid-fire guns were just being developed. All were mounted on various types of carriages and required

crews to serve them.

All artillery had made technological advances in several interrelated fields during the decades before the Civil War. Captain Thomas J. Rodman developed a new revolutionary process of casting cannon at the Fort Pitt Foundry in Pittsburgh. He cast guns around a water-cooled hollow core, thereby cooling the metal from the inside out, the reverse of cooling methods previously used.[3] This process permitted the fabrication of stronger and larger guns which, in turn, greatly affected ballistics qualities.

In the months before open hostilities, a former army officer, Robert Parker Parrott, superintendent of the West Point Foundry in

New York, developed a rifling system for artillery that was accepted by the military establishment and eventually used in rifled pieces of half a dozen calibers.[4] The Ordnance Department also had adopted a bronze smoothbore field gun developed by Louis Napoleon of France (1803-1873) as the Model 1857 12-Pounder Field Gun.[5] Nicknamed the "Napoleon," it became the most widely used field piece by both sides during the war. Concurrently, a number of patent breechloading systems were undergoing testing and field trials in the United States and abroad.

Powder had been greatly improved by a co-operative effort of Lammot du Pont of the Du Pont Company and Captain Rodman. Powders previously used exerted a blasting or disruptive force rather than a propelling force. Rodman developed a pressure gauge to measure the force of an explosion, and this took the guesswork of out

Above: Selection of field artillery projectiles. The two round balls are 6- and 12-pounder solid shot for smoothbore guns. All others were fired from 3- and 3.76-inch rifles. The top right round is a 3-inch Hotchkiss patent canister. The two odd-shaped projectiles are Schenkl patent shells. Others are Hotchkiss and Absterdam projectiles.

the manufacture of powder. Rodman and Du Pont developed Mammoth gunpowder that had various size grains depending upon the caliber of gun, and a controlled and predictable burning rate that acted as a propellant.[6] This new powder gave artillery greatly increased range, accuracy and penetrating power. The Du Pont Company put Mammoth gunpowder to immediate military use.

Various patent projectiles were developed for use in new rifled guns. Most had a soft metal base or band that was forced into the rifling of the piece by expanding gases during the moment of firing to impart spin to the projectile, thus enhancing both range and accuracy. Time fuzes for these projectiles enabled the artillerist to produce an airburst. Percussion fuzes were designed to produce detonation upon impact. But all fuzes, particularly Confederate ones, were undependable, and many projectiles failed to explode.

The early arsenals

Of the nine foundries casting cannon in 1860, seven were in the northern states and only two, the Tredegar Iron Works and Bellona Arsenal at Richmond, were in the south. Almost all of the powder mills in the country were located in northern states, the most important being the Du Pont Company near Wilmington, Delaware. There was only one major powder source in the south, located in Nashville, Tennessee, and a smaller facility in South Carolina. When the war began the Federal Army had an ample supply of modern artillery. The new Confederacy was forced to turn to the following sources of supply: cannon already in state or local militia hands (mostly obsolete types, about 400 guns); those guns captured during the initial occupation of former Federal installations, such as the Gosport Naval Yard in Norfolk, coastal forts and arsenals (about 1,750 guns, mostly large caliber seacoast guns); battlefield captures during the summer and fall of 1862 (about 250 current model light guns); and more than 125 foreign guns of various types that had been run through the blockade from England and the European continent.[7] The Federal Army also had the advantage of existing units of regular artillery that provided a small core of trained professional artillerists upon which to build. The Confederacy really had no similar trained units, only a few volunteer militia companies, and precious few soldiers who had ever served a gun.

All of the foundries, North and South, produced two basic types of artillery – smoothbores and rifles. Smoothbore cannon had been in service for years and were generally classified as guns, howitzers, mortars and columbiads. Guns had a flat trajectory and longer range. Howitzers had a higher trajectory but shorter range, while mortars had a very high trajectory and very short relative range. The big columbiads had characteristics of all three and were much larger caliber. Rifles were a new innovation and just gaining general acceptance because of their much longer range, greater accuracy and destructive power.

Gun crews

Serving a gun, regardless of the size of the piece, required a highly trained crew. Numbers varied depending on specific guns but a typical gun crew consisted of eight men – a gunner or gun captain and seven cannoneers. Each crew member was assigned a number and had a specific function, with every motion performed in a specified manner and proscribed order.

To put a gun into action on the command "Load," crew member Number 1 sponged the bore as Number 2 received from Number 5 the cartridge, a projectile with propellant bag attached, which he inserted into the muzzle of the piece. Number 1, who never let go of the rammer, pushed the round down the tube, seated it and withdrew the rammer, while Number 3 kept his thumb, protected by a padded leather thumbstall, over the vent. The gunner (the non-commissioned officer who aimed the piece, or the gun captain)

Below: A water battery at Pensacola, Florida, in 1861, opposite Ft. Pickens, shows Confederate gun crews still without uniforms manning Model 1841 32-pounder iron guns mounted on Model 1839 wood front pintle barbette carriages. The gun carriage swiveled on the pintle to allow the gun to engage different targets.

then stepped to the breech to sight the gun while Number 3 dropped back to the trail of the carriage to grasp the handspike to shift the cannon according to the gunner's or gun captain's directions. At the same time Number 5 returned to the limber a short distance behind the gun and received another round from Numbers 6 and 7, who had removed the round from the limber chest and already cut the fuze to the gunner's or gun captain's shouted order.

When the gun was aimed the latter stepped aside in order to observe the effect of fire and ordered "Ready." Quickly, Numbers 1 and 2 stood back from the muzzle and to the side of the wheels of the carriage. Number 3 pushed the priming wire or vent pick down the vent and perforated the propellant bag, exposing the black powder charge. Number 4 hooked a friction primer to the lanyard, a piece of stout cord with a hook at one end and a wooden grip on the other, and inserted the primer into the vent. Number 3 held the primer while Number 4 stepped back, keeping the lanyard slack. The gunner or gun captain ordered "Fire" as Number 3 stepped away from the wheel, and Number 4 pulled the lanyard, discharging the piece with a loud metallic "blank" accompanied by dense clouds of white smoke. The cannon recoiled violently half a dozen feet to the rear.

At the same time Number 5 delivered the next prepared round to Number 2 and the crew ran the gun back into battery, upon which the sequence was begun again.[8] There was no wasted effort or motion. Every movement of the deadly dance was done with style and grace. The rate of fire was dependent largely on the type of weapon and carriage because the tube had to be pointed and sighted after each discharge due to shifting during recoil.

Below: *Ammunition for field and siege artillery moving with the Army on campaign had to be transported in the Ordnance train. This required a detailed logistical plan by the ordnance officer in charge to insure wagon-load after wagon-load of adequate supplies of various caliber and types of projectiles were in close proximity to the appropriate batteries when needed.*

There was never-ending drill, whether in garrison or the field, because the crew had to function flawlessly regardless of the circumstances. Nothing could be allowed to distract them from the rhythm of serving the gun. In many battles, gun crews fought in the open without the protection of earthworks, embrasures and traverses. The crews often served their guns fully exposed to small arms fire of opposing infantry and counter-battery fire from enemy guns. They had unflinching resolve to stand in the way of a veritable hail of shot and exploding shell and methodically serve their piece.

Gun batteries

The basic artillery unit was the battery consisting, in Federal service but often not in the Confederate artillery, of six guns, usually the same caliber. Confederate batteries were reduced to four guns by mid war and never had fire superiority over comparable Federal units. Two gun sections – a battery wagon and field forge – were attached to each battery, which made the unit reasonable self-sufficient.

A captain usually commanded a battery, supported by four lieutenants, one as executive officer and the others as section commanders. There were fourteen non-commissioned officers, other support staff, and around 125 privates. A fully equipped battery boasted 155 officers and men, 52 of whom were drivers while 70 were gun crew. To move a battery required 72 horses – six per gun, plus horses to pull the battery wagon and field forge. In addition there were officers' mounts and replacements, about 112 animals.[9] These numbers were reduced by attrition as the war continued.

Field artillery accompanied every army in every campaign during the war and served in offensive and defensive capacities in Federal and Confederate armies. Confederate forces captured a considerable number

Below: Ammunition had to be brought to the gun from the ammunition chest on the limber stationed to the rear of the gun. The chest carried a mix of projectiles for specific targets and the number of rounds in the chest varied, based on the caliber of the gun. The Napoleon chest, for instance, carried 32 projectiles: 12 solid shot, 12 case shot, 4 shells and 4 canister. When all ammunition was expended the limber had to return to the ordnance train somewhere in the rear to replenish ammunition.

Above: *Cannon crews fought their guns in a very exposed manner. Armor and overhead cover had not yet been developed. Counter-battery fire was often deadly accurate and casualties resulted from wood splinters from shattered carriages as well as exploding shells. Many times guns were lost because all battery animals had been killed and there was no way to remove guns from harm's way. As a last resort the tube was spiked by driving a nail or wire into the vent to disable the gun.*

of Northern guns and used them during the war. The Napoleon, Parrott rifle and 3-inch Ordnance Rifle were so popular that Confederate ordnance facilities fabricated their own adaptations of these types throughout the war.

One of the most widely used field guns was the Model 1857 12-Pounder Gun, also called the Light 12-Pounder but best known North or South as the Napoleon. The bronze gun weighed just over 1,200 pounds, was easy to manufacture, relatively inexpensive and, above all, dependable. The 4.62-inch smoothbore Napoleon was deadly in broken, wooded country, the topography of most Civil War battlefields, where its 1,600-yard range was more than adequate. The gun fired solid shot, shell, spherical case and canister with ease and could be discharged with careful aim twice a minute. When pressed, a good crew firing canister could get off four rounds a minute.[10]

Just over 1,100 Napoleons were made for the Federal Ordnance Department by the Ames Manufacturing Company, Chicopee, Massachusetts, Cyrus Alger & Co., Revere Copper Company, and Henry N. Hooper & Co, Boston, and Miles Greenwood & Co., Cincinnati. Confederate Ordnance received about 501 Napoleons from government arsenals at Augusta, Columbus and Macon, Georgia, Charleston, South Carolina, and Tredegar Iron Works in Richmond, as well as several private foundries.

Both sides had considerable numbers of cannon made obsolete by the Napoleon and the new iron rifles. The Model 1841 6-Pounder Field Gun, was one of them. Federal Ordnance retired most of these guns from the field early in the war. The Confederates were forced by necessity to keep many of them in service even though it was immediately obvious they were hopelessly outgunned. Federal Ordnance did make an effort to upgrade some of these bronze guns by rifling them with special James rifling of fifteen lands (raised portion) and grooves, developed by General Charles Tillinghast James and firing his patent projectile.[11] These guns are properly referred to today as rifled 6-pounders. Regardless, they were no match for iron rifles and were relegated to western units or defensive positions in fixed fortifications.

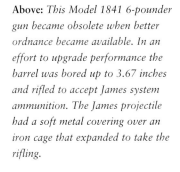

The Model 1861 3-inch Ordnance Rifle was manufactured by the Phoenix Iron Company of Phoenixville, PA, near Philadelphia, who delivered 1,100 of these wrought iron rifles during the war at a cost of less than $300 per gun. Similar pattern guns were made of cast steel in limited numbers by Singer-Nimick & Co., Pittsburgh, and purportedly of german silver[12] by Henry N. Hooper & Co, Boston, These sleek guns weighed just over 800 pounds and had a range of 4,000 yards. Their safety record ranked with that of the Napoleon with only one recorded as burst in action. Brigadier General Edward Porter Alexander, Chief of Ordnance, Army of Northern Virginia,

Above: *This Model 1841 6-pounder gun became obsolete when better ordnance became available. In an effort to upgrade performance the barrel was bored up to 3.67 inches and rifled to accept James system ammunition. The James projectile had a soft metal covering over an iron cage that expanded to take the rifling.*

Left: *The wrought iron 3-inch Ordnance rifle was one of the finest field artillery pieces of the war. Light, safe, accurate and maneuverable, it was effective in every of situation. The 3-inch Hotchkiss and Schenkl rounds performed particularly well with this rifle. The limber and chest is standard size but the interior layout of the chest was specifically made to handle 3-inch projectiles.*

referred to them as "the beautiful United States Three Inch Ordnance Rifles."[13] Tredegar Iron Works, Noble Brothers & Co, Rome, Georgia, and several smaller foundries made limited numbers of this pattern. It was immensely popular with artillerists of both armies. An ordnance rifle of Captain Samuel Elder's Battery B, 1st U.S. Artillery, Number 100, was said to have fired the last artillery round of the Civil War at Appomattox, April 9, 1865.[14] Postwar efforts to convert the weapon to a breechloading gun were not satisfactory and many were scrapped.

The Parrott Rifle

Robert Parker Parrott, a former ordnance officer, patented his namesake rifle in 1861. At his West Point Foundry, under his direct supervision, he manufactured models in at least six different calibers for the Army and Navy during the war. His rifle had a cast iron barrel with an applied wrought iron reinforcing band at the breech. It was cheap, could be produced quickly in quantity and was easy to operate by inexperienced gunners. Parrotts did have problems with bursting, especially the larger guns. As Parrott himself quickly acknowledged, his gun wasn't the best, but it was good enough and already in production, and available immediately.[15] The State of Virginia had ordered thirteen in 1860 and other states, North and South, bought these modern rifled guns from Parrott before the war. Field guns of the Parrott system were the 10-pounder, the early version having 2.9-inch bore, the 1863 model with 3-inch bore, and the 20-pounder 3.67-inch rifle. The 3-inch weighed 890 pounds, while the 3.67-inch weighed a hefty 1,750 and was considered too small for a siege gun but too heavy for convenient use as a field gun.

Nevertheless, a 3.67-inch Parrott Rifle with a competent crew could easily hit a target at 2,500 yards, about twice the range of the Napoleon.[16] Confederate Ordnance saw immediately the ease of production of this pattern rifle. Tredegar made fifty-eight 10-Pounder Parrotts and forty-five 20-pounder Parrotts during the war, and Macon Arsenal made 10-, 20- and 30-pounders for the Army of Tennessee, although these were unsatisfactory. Several other private contractors made limited numbers of varying quality.[17] Ultimately, the Parrott was recognized as a simple, rugged and effective weapon with some faults, filling a need but never achieving the popularity of the Ordnance Rifle.

Norman Wiard, a Canadian, held the post of Superintendent of Ordnance Stores for the Army. He was a prolific inventor with many novel ideas and was in the right position to advance his theories for a radically different ordnance system. Wiard designed a small, lightweight iron gun in both rifled and smoothbore formats, using what he called semi-steel, a low carbon cast iron. The three types were a 2.6-inch rifle, 3.6-inch rifle and a 12-pounder 4.62-inch smoothbore howitzer.[18] He also developed a unique carriage that greatly reduced length of recoil, facilitated easy maintenance and repair, and allowed for high elevation of the barrel. Wiard is said to have sold only eleven batteries, some sixty-six pieces.[19] Apparently, his was an excellent but unconventional weapons system that never attained the popularity and acceptance of the Napoleon, Ordnance and Parrott rifles.

The Confederacy imported some interesting English cannon in limited numbers. The Whitworth 6-pounder 2.17-inch and 12-pounder 2.75-inch, breechloading rifles were some of the most fascinating and expensive cannon of the war. Developed by Sir Joseph Whitworth, these guns were made by the Whitworth Ordnance Company in Manchester, England, and run through the Federal blockade. The barrel was made of steel and had hexagonal rifling. Projectiles, both shot and shell, were machined to fit the rifling, giving the piece a range of 10,000 yards and uncanny accuracy. The English carriage was very heavy and usually was replaced by a more standard field carriage. Unfortunately, the breech mechanism tended to malfunction with rough field use and obtaining the required special ammunition was always a

Below: Both Union and Confederate armies used the light, portable Coehorn mortar as a close support weapon. Four good men were capable of carrying it forward for short distances in an assault and the high angle of fire was ideal for lobbing explosive rounds over the parapet of a fort or entrenched position. Of course, other personnel had to carry sufficient powder and projectiles to serve the piece. The Federal Model 1841 brass 5.82-inch or 24-pounder Coehorn (left) weighed about 200 pounds including the wooden bed. The Confederate iron Coehorn of the same caliber with bed weighed slightly more.

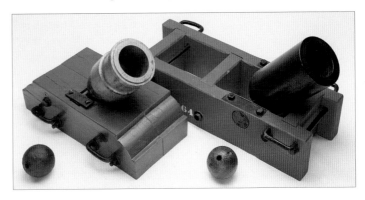

Below: *The Model 1841 Mountain Howitzer had a 4.62-inch smoothbore. The little bronze gun was less than four feet long. Its short range was a decided disadvantage but it was capable of firing a 12-pounder canister which was deadly close up. Most of these howitzers were relegated to the western theater in areas of broken wooded terrain where there were not long fields of fire. Carried disassembled on pack mules, the gun could go almost anywhere.*

problem. Confederate Ordnance was able to manufacture Whitworth ammunition in Richmond that performed well with the guns. Other calibers were imported in even smaller numbers.[20]

The Federal Army had a small bronze Coehorn mortar, Model 1841. While not a field piece, it was highly mobile and was used as a close support weapon. The pattern was originally developed about 1670 by the famed Dutch engineer, Baron van Menno Corhoorn.[21] The Confederates had their own cast iron version of the weapon. The small mortar weighed only 300 pounds and was fitted with handles that allowed four men to carry it with relative ease for short distances. It could lob an explosive shell over a parapet and was very effective.

The Model 1841 Mountain Howitzer, a 12-pounder smoothbore bronze gun, was used in two configurations. It could be broken down and carried on pack mules when operating in rough terrain, or mounted on a light prairie carriage pulled by two horses in tandem for use on the plains. The barrel weighed only 220 pounds. The little gun had a very short range, effectively just about 900 yards and any bigger counter-battery fire could just stay 1,000 yards or more out and pound the ineffective smaller gun to pieces at will. It was regarded as an infantry close support weapon. It saw little use in the East but Confederates in the western theater used them with enough success that Tredegar Iron Works cast a limited number of them.[22] The mountain howitzer was best used against the American Indian who lacked any artillery at all during and after the war.

Siege and fortification artillery

The categories of siege and fortification artillery and seacoast artillery basically refer to the same large guns but with different applications. All were characterized by great size and weight, leading thus to difficulty of movement, large caliber and devastating effect. Rate of fire was much slower with the big guns but they could fire 12 rounds per hour and were capable when pressed of 20 rounds an hour, but not for sustained periods.[23] Carriages of pieces varied considerably depending upon the fortification and offensive or defensive use of the gun

The 30-pounder 4.2-inch Parrott Rifle, weighing about 4,200

pounds, and the Model 1861 4.5-inch siege rifle, weighing about 3,500 pounds, were the smallest siege guns. Both guns were transported upon a siege and garrison carriage that required the barrel being mounted before going into action and then dismounted again for travel.[24] One of these 4.2-inch Parrotts mounted at Cummings Point fired at Charleston, at a range of 6,600 yards, for sixty-nine days before bursting on the 4,553rd shot, an enviable record of endurance.[25] Parrott also made a 100-pounder which was used extensively in fixed fortifications on a center pintle carriage that allowed a 360 degree field of fire. The "Swamp Angel," a 200-pounder behind Morris Island, burst on the 36th discharge while shelling Charleston at a range of 8,000 yards, while a 300-pounder rifle weighing nearly 27,000 pounds and with a 10-inch bore was also made in limited numbers toward the end of the war.

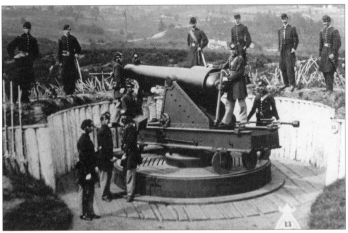

Columbiads – large iron guns, originally smoothbore with some banded and rifled during the war – were the primary coastal fortification armament. Their heavy caliber, long range and high elevation made them ideal guardians of channels and harbors. Rodman Columbiads with 8-, 10-, 15- and 20-inch bores were made. The 20-inch Model 1864 weighed 115,000 pounds and fired a 1,000-pound projectile about 8,000 yards. None of the 15-inch guns and the few 20-inch guns ever fired a shot in anger and spent postwar years until the 1890s silently guarding the coastal areas.[26] The smaller 8- and 10-inch guns of both Federal and Confederate manufacture were used extensively during the war.

Obsolete smoothbore guns such as the Model 1839 18-pounder, Model 1819 24-pounder, Model 1829 32-pounder, and Model 1841 42-pounder saw much use in fixed fortifications North and South.

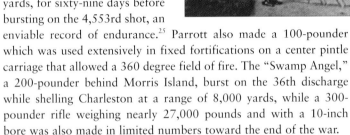

Above: *This Model 1861 6.4-inch Parrott Rifle is mounted on a Model 1859 wrought iron center pintle barbette carriage at Fort Stevens, another of the fortifications surrounding Washington, D.C. This carriage had been designed for 8- and 10-inch Columbiads but was modified to accept several caliber Parrott rifles. A large screw mechanism at the breech of the gun facilitated elevation. The gun crew's shoulder arms with fixed bayonets are shown leaning against the white washed wood wall of the gun pit.*

Above: *A gun crew of the 1st Connecticut Heavy Artillery man a Model 1841 32-pounder gun mounted on a wood siege and garrison carriage. Note that Number 1 is sponging the bore while another member of the crew stands ready to hand him the rammer to load cartridge. The gun appears to be in full recoil position having just been fired. The gun captain is crouched behind the gun, sighting the piece, while another crew member stands ready with a handspike should the piece need to be traversed.*

One of the most interesting of these was the gun at Vicksburg and known by both sides as "Whistling Dick."[27] The piece made history on May 27, 1863, when one of its screaming shells sank the Union gunboat *Cincinnati*. For many years the gun had been misidentified but it is now believed to be an old Model 1839 18-pounder iron siege/garrison gun, made at the Tredegar Iron Works before the war and rifled and banded by Confederate Ordnance.

Many of these older models were mounted on barbette carriages, either front or center pintle, depending on their mission. Large howitzers were also used in defensive roles in many fortifications, particularly for flank defense. The 8-inch siege and garrison howitzer, Model 1841, firing canister rounds containing forty-eight balls, was very effective at dispersing any assaulting force.

Large mortars, 8- and 10-inch siege pieces and 10- and 13-inch seacoast pieces, Models 1841 and 1861, saw considerable use. A number of large mortars were use in the siege lines before Yorktown in 1862. The man-hours expended to dig emplacements, bring the mortars in and mount them, only to have Confederate forces withdraw before they could begin firing, was frustrating to say the least. To increase mobility, a 13-inch monster, known as "The Dictator," weighing over 17,000 pounds, was mounted on a railway flat car on the Petersburg and City Point Railroad in 1864. Recoil of the mortar moved the car some ten or twelve feet down the track but the 218-pound shell arced over 4,200 yards into the besieged Confederate lines with demoralizing effect.[28] Confederates copied the Model 1841 series and had seized a substantial number of large mortars at the beginning of the war. Their use of mortars was limited and primarily defensive.

Left: *This huge Model 1861 13-inch seacoast mortar, known as "The Dictator," has been mounted on a specially strengthened railway platform car with eight wheels so that it can be moved along the Petersburg and City Point Railroad within the Union siege line to shell different positions in beleaguered Petersburg. When the monster was fired the car moved 10 to 12 feet on down the line. These same mortars were mounted on barges and schooners for special work. "The Dictator" is mounted at Hartford, Connecticut, today.*

Imported heavy artillery

Importation through the blockade of heavy English ordnance provided the Confederacy with some of the most advanced pattern guns available. Four 70-pounder 5-inch Whitworth rifles, costing 700 pounds sterling, were brought over but were captured aboard the blockade runner *Princess Royal* by Union forces and used against the intended recipients at Morris Island, South Carolina.[29] A considerable number of larger cannon using Blakely's hook-slant rifling in 4-inch up to a huge 12.75-inch were secured from several English firms. The latter were the biggest rifles in the Confederacy, weighing 60,480 pounds and measuring 16 feet 2-inches in length. The most famous is the "Widow Blakely," originally a British 42-pounder that was reworked by Blakely at Low Moor into a 7.5-inch banded and rifled gun and sent on to the South. It was part of the Vicksburg defenses during the siege, and was captured and taken to West Point. It was returned to Vicksburg in 1959.[30]

The finest big gun in the Confederate arsenal was the 8-inch muzzleloading Armstrong rifle. Two of these magnificent rifles came into the port of Wilmington on the blockade runner *Hope* on September 3, 1864. One was placed at Fort Fisher.[31] The rifle was

Right: *This fine English rifle is known as a 150-pounder Armstrong or 8-inch Armstrong. It is mounted on an English barbette carriage. Both rifle and carriage, together with implements and a supply of projectiles, were run through the Federal blockade from St. George, Bermuda, in 1864. This piece became part of the main armament at Fort Fisher, North Carolina, guarding the port of Wilmington. The barrel weighs 15,737 pounds. Note successive steps on the barrel. The central tube was actually made of steel with successive wrought iron bands formed around a mandrel shrunk over the breech.*

captured there on January 15, 1865, and now resides on Trophy Point at the West Point Military Academy. Two other 8-inch Armstrong rifles bought by the Confederacy never made it to southern shores but were left in Bermuda and sold at public auction in November 1865 to satisfy Confederate debts on the island.[32]

Movement of these massive guns required considerable power and effort by man and beast. Confederate Ordnance developed a sling cart with wheels about 11 feet in diameter and required twelve mules and 150 men to manage it. The gun tube was carried just inches off the ground, roads permitting. Federal artillery moved their big guns on low-slung, four-wheel carts pulled by at least eight pairs of mules and oxen. The work was dangerous and tedious, and speed was never a factor.[33]

Rapid-fire weapons

Visionary individuals on both sides saw the potential of rapid-fire weapons to increase firepower. Experiments before the war had been unsuccessful but enterprising men continued development despite the ignorance of senior ordnance officers. Significant developments occurred on both sides during the war.

Dr. Richard Jordan Gatling was the inventor of the first truly successful machine gun used in warfare. After initial production was lost in a fire, Gatling had subsequent guns made at the Cincinnati

Type Foundry in 1863. The gun design was a hand-crank-operated weapon with six steel barrels revolving around a central shaft. The .58 caliber paper cartridges loaded into steel cylinders with percussion nipples on the back end were gravity fed to the gun from a brass hopper mounted on top of the breech. As the crank was turned six cam-operated bolts alternately chambered, fired and ejected the cylinders, which could be collected and reloaded with regular-issue paper cartridges and re-used in later engagements. The gun was somewhat air-cooled by the revolving motion of the barrels. The projected rate of fire was six hundred rounds per minute, solely dependent on strength and stamina of the operator.

Sometimes faulty alignment, fragile chambers and radical design dissuaded any government interest but Gatling managed to sell twelve guns at $1,000.00 each to Major-General Benjamin Butler, well known for his own eccentric ideas, and one to Admiral David Dixon Porter, all mounted on field carriages. These Gatling guns were used in front of Petersburg in 1864.[34] In August 1866, the U.S. Army became the first in the world to adopt a "machine gun," an improved version, and subsequently considerable numbers in various calibers were sold all over the world into the 20th century. The basic design is used in modern aircraft machine guns and cannon that have a very high cyclical rate of fire.

The Billinghurst-Requa Battery Gun consisted of twenty-five .54 caliber barrels mounted parallel to each other and laid horizontally on a light metal field carriage. It was built by Billinghurst Company of Rochester, New York, in late 1861. A clip holding twenty-five metallic cartridges was fitted onto a sliding bar operated by two levers that chambered the

Below: The Billinghurst-Requa Battery Gun was one of the more novel and bizarre weapons systems to come out of the war, an excellent example of a fertile mind. While the idea eventually became an impractical dead end it served to spur others in different directions in the quest for more firepower. The photograph shows the weapon with the covers open and barrels exposed, ready for loading. The clips or magazines are lying on the ground. One of the raised loading levers can be seen. While the weapon was not a resounding success it did point the way for those to follow.

cartridges in their respective barrels. A train of powder then had to be poured in a narrow tray across the breech and ignited with a single percussion cap, a simple operation allowing use by unskilled crew.[35] The gun had a projected rate of fire of seven volleys or 175 shots per minute, with an effective range of 1,300 yards in theory. Regrettably, damp weather fouled the powder in the semi-exposed tray and often rendered the gun useless. It was suggested that the weapon would be ideal for guarding restricted approaches such as covered bridges, thus earning it the sobriquet "covered bridge gun." Several saw field use in South Carolina campaigns. Reports indicated that rapid fouling and overheating were major objections to this design, The battery gun had the distinction of being the first clip-fed, metallic-cartridge, rapid-fire gun used in actual combat.[36]

The Union Repeating Gun, also known as the Ager Coffee Mill Gun, was a single-barreled gun mounted on light artillery carriage. Atop the gun was a brass hopper that was manually filled with steel cartridge cases that dropped into a revolving cylinder actuated by a hand crank. The steel cartridge cases were hand loaded with .58 caliber paper cartridges and became prepared ammunition. As the case cycled through the gun it was fired and the empty case ejected to the ground where it could be recovered and reloaded. As with the Gatling, rate of fire depended upon the strong arm of the operator. The gun, with its lone barrel, was prone to overheat quickly.

President Abraham Lincoln examined one of these weapons in a carriage shop near Willard's Hotel with salesman J. D. Mills of New York in June 1861 and later saw it fired at the Washington Arsenal. The president was so impressed that he ordered ten guns that October after the Ordnance Department showed no interest. On December 19, 1861, Major General George B. McClellan bought an additional fifty and two of these were in the field in January 1862 with the 28th Pennsylvania Volunteer Infantry who were thought to have used them in a skirmish around Harpers Ferry. At Middleburg, Virginia, on March 29, 1862, a Captain Bartlett noted that a "Coffee Mill" gun was fired at Confederate cavalry at 800 yards, cutting it to pieces and forcing survivors to flee, and the 56th New York Infantry had six of them at Yorktown in April 1862. The Confederates captured seventeen at Harpers Ferry in September 1862 and in 1864 used one near Reams' Station, Virginia, to fire at a Union observation balloon, conceivably making it the first anti-aircraft gun.[37]

Confederate rapid-fire guns

Confederate inventors were active in the field, if slightly less successful. Pate, Tappey and Lumsden of Petersburg, Virginia, built two 4-pounder revolving cannon with high expectations of bringing death and destruction to all the Yankees. It was basically a giant, crank-operated, five-shot, smoothbore revolver on a carriage that resembled a piece of farm equipment, evidently of too light construction. The first gun burst during tests in May 1861 and the project was abruptly canceled.[38]

The Vandenburgh Volley Gun was the brainchild of General Origen Vandenburgh of the New York State Militia. In 1860, he endeavored unsuccessfully to interest English ordnance in his idea, but Robinson and Cottam of London made guns of this pattern. The governor of North Carolina allegedly purchased one gun and legend has it that two were run through the blockade. One gun, Number 4, had eighty-five .50 caliber barrels clustered in a brass housing and, although only 36 inches long, the barrel cluster weighed 400 pounds. Federal Cavalry captured this gun near Salisbury, North Carolina, in April, 1865.[39] The other gun had one hundred and twenty-one .45 caliber barrels in the brass housing and may have been part of the armament of the garrison at Fort Fisher, North Carolina. The barrels were clustered, row upon row, in a cylindrical barrel housing that had the appearance of a honeycomb. When the breechblock was unscrewed and open a "magazine" with all the charges was inserted, the block closed and locked, and a single percussion hammer set off

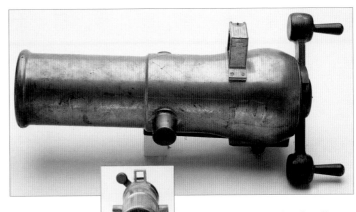

Above: *The Vandenburgh Volley Gun was a Yankee invention, manufactured in England and bought by a Confederate. It also was a novel idea that went somewhat astray. It was quite heavy for its size, awkward to reload and, because of lack of projectile dispersion, did not really accomplish its intended task. All the firepower was concentrated in one small area. It remains today at the West Point Museum as another curiosity in the quest for firepower.*

the whole thing. It was obviously painfully slow to load even with pre-loaded magazines ready, and because of the close barrel alignment there was little dispersion, as in canister shot.[40]

The Williams rapid-fire gun was actually quite successful and saw real service in both eastern and western theaters of the war. The gun was the invention of R. S. Williams of Kentucky who oversaw its production at the Tredegar Iron Works. The cannon saw action at the Battle of Seven Pines in 1862 and performance was so favorable that the War Department authorized Williams to raise a battery armed with his gun. Tredegar produced 20 of them in 1862-1863 and Samson and Pae, also of Richmond, turned out another four Williams guns. Two full batteries were established at Lynchburg, Virginia, and another at Mobile. The gun was a one-pounder, steel breechloader with a two inch bore, and mounted on a two-wheeled field carriage light enough to be pulled by one horse. The hand crank was attached to a revolving camshaft that rotated a cylinder below a hopper holding the ammunition. A gunner operated the crank that opened the breech and cocked the hammer, while another member of the crew inserted the cartridge and capped the nipple. Closing the breech tripped the hammer and fired the gun. A third man sighted the gun during the firing cycle. Theoretical rate of fire was about 20 rounds per minute, and range was 2,000 yards.[41]

The wide array of ordnance used during the Civil War fired no fewer than seventy different kinds of projectiles, and supply was an ordnance officer's nightmare. Smoothbore guns fired solid shot, shell that burst into fragments, case shot that burst into fragments, and also scattered missiles packed within (what is now called shrapnel after the inventor British Lieutenant, later General, Henry Shrapnel in 1784) and canister – light metal cans filled with lead or iron missiles. Rifles fired elongated solid shot called bolts, as well as shell, case and canister of similar form. Most rifle projectiles were named after the inventor, such as Parrott, Schenkl, Dyer, Hotchkiss, Absterdam, Sawyer and James, and were manufactured in a host of calibers.

Advances in metallurgy and propellants greatly increased range, accuracy and destructive power of large caliber guns and foretold the end of masonry forts as an effective defense. These improvements in the art of war led to the development of elaborate earth and sand emplacements that could absorb and neutralize the effect of heavy artillery. Artillery became the impetus of elaborate earthworks and entrenchments to get the soldiers below the ground. Experimentation would continue with breechloading guns but they would not be accepted by the establishment until the end of the century. Development of field artillery was stagnant to the degree that the United States Army was dependent on French models a half a century later during Word War I. Alert military minds saw the potential of rapid-fire guns, and Gatling continued to improve his models, but the true machine gun was still years ahead.

Left: *Confederate- and English-manufactured projectiles for field artillery pieces. Most are variations of Read or Parrott shells for 3-inch rifles. The two hexagonal projectiles in the foreground are an English Whitworth 2.75-inch shell and a bolt or shot. The small round between them is speculatively identified as a projectile for the Williams 2-inch rapid-fire gun. Several of the projectiles have obvious bourrelets, raised bearing surfaces, that facilitated ease and speed of manufacture. Only the bearing surfaces were lathe-turned to fit the bore, greatly reducing production time.*

CHAPTER FOUR

Other Equipment

*To enter a Sibley tent whose flaps had been closed on a cold night
". . . and encounter the night's accumulation of nauseating exhalations from
the bodies of twelve men was an experience which no old soldier
has ever been known to recall with great enthusiasm."*
(John D. Billings, Massachusetts artilleryman, in *Hardtack and Coffee*)

MILITARY INFORMATION AND communications on the battlefield were of paramount importance during the Civil War. In a time before the luxury of instant radio-telephone contact other methods of direction and control were used to direct troop movements and issue orders.

The Union Army's Signal Corps existed in an unofficial capacity at the beginning of the war but was not officially approved until March 3, 1863. Colonel Benjamin Franklin Fisher is acknowledged as the "father of the Signal Corps," which eventually mustered 300 officers and 2,500 enlisted ranks during the war.[1] Personnel of the corps eventually had special insignia in the form of crossed signal flags worn in a wreath on headgear for officers and on both sleeves of enlisted ranks.[2]

Signalmen played an important role in every campaign. Had it not been for a Federal signal station at Sugar Loaf, Maryland, General Lee's 1862 invasion of Maryland would have been a complete surprise. And a signal station on Little Round Top at Gettysburg on the second day of the battle gave advance warning of the Confederate intent to occupy the hill and enfilade the whole Federal line.

Signal messages were sent by means of flags, torches or lights. The latter were Coston lights that were used with special signal pistols. Different colors and combinations of colors were used to send prearranged signals. Flags and torches were used to send messages by

Above: *Signal stations sprung up on prominent terrain features surrounding Washington and followed the armies during campaigns. The Federal Signal Corps, loosely organized at first, became a bona fide military organization by mid-war. Signalmen in gray never quite achieved such autonomous status.*

"wig-wag" movement. Some messages were encoded using a cipher disk. Not only did the corps send messages but its men gathered intelligence by interception and translation of messages sent by opposing signalmen.

Captain (later General) E. P. Alexander was the first Signal Officer of the Confederate Army of Northern Virginia. Southern signalmen were attached to the Adjutant-General's Department. Upon Alexander's promotion and transfer Captain (later Colonel) William Norris commanded the Confederate Signal Corps which was responsible for not only signaling but also telegraphy and secret-service work. Gray-clad signalmen used much the same equipment as their northern counterparts – cipher disks, flags and torches.[3]

Telegraphy

The Federal Army had the Military Telegraph Service traveling in the field. The quasi-military organization employed civilian operators and utilized existing commercial systems, but also constructed more than fifteen thousand miles of dedicated military telegraph wire. This unsung group of men was a tactical factor in planning and execution of every military operation, and their opportune "tapping" of Confederate wires proved a very effective source of intelligence. The service enabled General Grant to keep under direct control military forces exceeding 500,000 men operating over a territory of eight hundred thousand square miles. And General Sherman said, "The value of the telegraph cannot be exaggerated as illustrated by the perfect accord of action of the armies in Virginia and Georgia."[4]

Confederate use of the telegraph was nowhere near as extensive as that of their antagonist. Interior lines of communication did not require the massive wire laying effort made by the Federal armies on

Below: Confederate telegraph components. The larger object mounted on a wood base is a telegraph relay used by the Army of Northern Virginia. Below it are two brass cipher disks for decoding and encoding messages. The open wooden clamshell case is a pocket telegraph relay. Confederate telegraphers did become very adept at tapping into Federal wires and garnered considerable intelligence in that manner. Often they created confusion by sending spurious information over the wires, to the consternation of their opposite numbers.

the move. Nevertheless, aggressive wire-tapping by southern operators allowed the Confederates to acquire essential intelligence at various times during the conflict.

Aerial observation

Observation balloons, although used on a limited scale, foretold of the future of aerial observation and air bombardment. Balloons had been known for some years but it took the peculiar genius of cross-eyed Major General Benjamin F. Butler to perceive their use as an instrument of war. Butler sponsored John LaMountain of Troy, New York, who on August 1, 1862, attached a gas-filled balloon to the armed transport *Fanny* at Fortress Monroe, arguably making this vessel the first aircraft carrier. In the first night aerial reconnaissance, LaMountain was able to count the number of tent fires in surrounding Confederate camps and report estimated strengths. This necessitated a "black-out" by the Confederate forces.[5]

But it was Professor Thaddeus Sobieski Constantine Lowe who established the Federal Balloon Corps and became its first chief. Lowe flew his balloon over Washington and telegraphed a message from it to President Abraham Lincoln, thus carrying out the first air to ground communication. Some reporters later said that the president made a balloon ascent with Lowe. There is no question that Generals McClellan, Heintzelman, Stoneman and a then-junior officer, George Armstrong Custer, actually went up with Professor Lowe. There is also no question that the Army of the Potomac was provided with timely intelligence during the Peninsula Campaign in 1862, unfortunately for that army with negligible results.[6]

Below: *Professor Lowe, standing to the immediate right of the balloon with his hand on it, supervises inflation of the craft by his ground crew before going aloft near Gaines Mill during the Peninsula Campaign. Lowe was easily the most experienced of the aerial observers of the period, with many hours in the air. Balloon flight was usually tethered and controlled from the ground unless the balloon accidentally broke free, which happened from time to time. Planned free flight from point to point was still in the future.*

Lowe had three balloons, the *Constitution*, *Intrepid*, and *Washington*. He used a converted coal barge, grandly named USS *George Washington Parke Custis*, as a mobile base. In an ascent near Arlington, Virginia, in August 1861, Lowe was fired on by an artillery piece dug into the ground so that the muzzle of the gun was elevated high enough to shoot at the pesky balloon, possibly the first use of anti-aircraft fire. Another Federal balloonist placed iron plate on the bottom of the basket in which he rode as protection from ground fire, and ascended with bombs and grenades, but with regrettably unreported effect – the first aerial bombardment.[7] Unfortunately, the Balloon Corps was disbanded in June 1863 because of the rigid, unimaginative minds of the military. The corps served in both eastern and western theaters, with a maximum of six balloons.

Confederate Captain John Randolph Bryan (given the nickname "Balloon" Bryan), aide-de-camp of General John B. Magruder, went up in a Confederate balloon over Yorktown and reported valuable information to General Johnston on the dispositions of Federal troops. Another balloon used during the Seven Days' battles was described by General Longstreet as a "great patchwork ship of many varied hues." Federals captured it on a steamer that went aground in the James River, and when the boys in blue gathered it in they supposedly got the last silk dresses in the Confederacy.[8]

Entrenchments

The dramatic improvements in artillery and small arms made a profound impression on the soldiers in blue and gray. The common soldier knew almost immediately that the days of the stand-up fight and massed frontal assault were almost over. Officers, professional and volunteer, were much slower to come to this conclusion, resulting in needless casualties. The obvious result of this realization was the construction of sophisticated earthworks and entrenchments whenever the opportunity arose. While the soldiers griped about the labor involved, they lost no time getting below ground away from murderous small arms and artillery fire. As the war wore on, entrenchments and fortifications became more and more elaborate,

Above: *Thaddeus Lowe had the foresight to realize that aerial observation needed to have mobility to be truly effective. He converted a coal barge to act as a floating base of operations (calling it the first aircraft carrier may be a small stretch of the imagination), and proceeded to launch his balloon above the Potomac River near Washington, D.C.*

Above: *The art of trench warfare improved overnight, as a direct result of great strides in ordnance technology.*

Below: *One of the great strides was the development of grenades. Thought was given to fragmentation, delayed ignition and safety.*

with defense in depth and systems of anti-personnel entanglements, abatis, wire, mines and fallen trees surrounding strongpoints.

Artillery was also "dug in" whenever possible. Embrasures in front of cannon were masked with mats when the gun wasn't in action and underground bombproofs for the protection of the gunners were constructed adjacent to batteries.[9] Confederate authorities even hired slave labor to dig fortifications around Richmond.

Grenades

Not surprisingly, these advances in fortifications spawned the development of special weapons that could greatly assist in the assault or defense of these positions. Hand grenades, in some form, usually small explosive spherical objects, had been used as a defensive measure since the 17th century. In the past a fuze was lit and the projectile dropped or rolled down onto the opposing force. In June 1861 William F. Ketchum of Buffalo, New York, patented a grenade that was thrown like a dart. The nose of the device had a striker inserted in it that struck a percussion cap seated on a cone within the body of the grenade and which detonated the interior charge upon impact. In theory it worked quite well. Men of the 4th Massachusetts and 110th New York assaulted Confederate positions at Port Hudson, Louisiana, using Ketchum grenades. To their chagrin, the Confederates made great sport of catching the flying grenades in blankets and throwing them back down onto their attackers in the ditch in front of the parapet. The optimistic Ketchum made three sizes of his grenade: the one-, three- and five-pound models, all fitted with paper fins attached to a short wooden shaft. The Ordnance Department bought a total of 93,200. Examples have been recovered at Petersburg, Vicksburg, Port Hudson, in Kentucky, and on the USS *Cairo* which was raised from the Yazoo River.

The Adams grenade, patented by John S. Adams of Taunton, Massachusetts, was another type purchased by the government. It consisted of a six-pounder shell with a paper time fuze activated by a friction primer attached to an 18-inch lanyard. When the grenadier threw the missile the lanyard activated the five-second fuze. It does not seem to have been particularly well received since there were no further purchases.

The Hanes grenade invented by W. E. Hanes of Covington, Kentucky, in 1862 was quite unusual. It was a sphere within a sphere. The inner sphere contained a powder charge and was studded with twelve to fourteen percussion caps on brass nipples. The outer sphere screwed together and any point of impact supposedly acted as an anvil. They were obviously very dangerous when armed. The army never made any purchases.

However, Confederate Ordnance manufactured a grenade at Augusta Arsenal that was similar to the Ketchum in many respects. Rather than a percussion striker it utilized one of the Raines Sensitive Primers developed by General Gabriel Raines, commandant of the Torpedo Bureau. These primers exploded under the slightest pressure.[10]

Above: *Brevet Maj. Gen. Henry L. Abbott, authority and cataloger of ordnance development, saw the Adams grenade at the Petersburg front and favored it over the Ketchum grenade. No unexploded Adams grenades, or identifiable grenade fragments, have been found on any battlefield.*

Below: *The period song "Tenting Tonight On The Old Camp Ground" was sung by veterans whose memories of tent life had dimmed with time or were slightly skewed. Communal living in a tent was not glorious; varying personal hygiene was always a problem.*

Tents

Whether in garrison or in the field the soldier had to sleep somewhere and his home for three seasons of the year was usually some kind of tent, a considerable variety of which appeared in the summer of 1861. Some units like the famed Washington Artillery of New Orleans came with colorful

candy-striped tents, but others showed up with no shelter at all. Wall tents were initially popular. These were canvas dwellings shaped exactly like a small house, but they were expensive and cumbersome to pitch and carry, and eventually were used as field hospitals and headquarters tents.

The Sibley tent, named for its inventor Henry H. Sibley, by now a brigadier general in the Confederate service, was more popular. It resembled an Indian teepee, a tall cone of canvas supported by a center pole. Flaps on the sides could be opened for ventilation, and an iron Sibley stove somewhat heated the interior. Often more than twenty men inhabited a single tent, spread out like the spokes of a wheel. Some soldiers found the Sibley healthier and more comfortable than regular barracks, but only on pleasant days. When the cold or rain forced the men to keep the tent flaps closed overnight, the air inside became unbearable. Eventually, the Sibley tent also proved too cumbersome for extensive field operations.

Tents became simpler, lighter, and as a rule less comfortable. For a time Billy Yank tried sleeping in the wedge tent. Exceedingly simple, it was little more than a six-foot length of canvas that its four to six occupants draped over a center pole. Stakes held its sides to the ground and end flaps closed the openings. With the ridge-pole only five feet off the ground, even the shorter soldiers were forced to stoop to enter. Each man had about seven square feet of space on the ground.

The dog tent, or pup tent as it was later called, patterned after the French Tente d'Abri, was issued during the latter part of 1862.[11] Two men shared it, and it took two men to make it, each one carrying with him a shelter half. They buttoned their halves together, slung the combination over a center pole, and then lay down side by side in the cramped interior.

Below: *Ingenious efforts were made to make the uncomfortable bearable. This Sibley tent has been raised off the ground about three feet by a wooden stockade wall, and a wood door has been fitted to replace the tent fly. It is possible this modification reduced drafts under the sides of the tent and through the flap, and certainly increased head room considerably.*

Confederates suffered continually from want of proper shelters. Captured Yankee tents, rubber ground cloths and blankets were greatly prized. Lacking tents, the Southerners improvised crude shelters of brush or fence rails with oil-cloths or canvas stretched over frameworks to make so-called "shebangs." However crude, they were reported by the inhabitants to be "very comfortable in warm weather."[12]

It was the fourth season of the year that became truly miserable for everyone. Units went into winter quarters for the really inclement months. Armed with axes and saws from company wagons, soldiers in blue and gray built huts and cabins with considerable skill and ingenuity, and laid them out with company streets complete with officer's quarters. Before the ground froze, they dug into the earth a foot or so, then built their log walls another four or five feet above the pit, capping them with roofs of brush or boards, or even tents slung over a center pole. Interior fires were common, with chimneys made of barrels or wattle. However, periods of rain and snow turned a winter camp into a veritable quagmire.

Military bands

Bands and martial music have always been an integral part of the military establishment. At the beginning of the war almost every northern regiment brought its own band into service. These men were paid non-combatants and were soon seen as needless expense. General Order 91 in July 1862 ordered all regimental bands mustered out within thirty days or consolidated into brigade bands. Nevertheless, an estimated fifty regimental bands remained in service after that date. About a hundred brigade bands served throughout the war.

Above left: *These wall tents have taken on a semi-permanent appearance, with brick chimneys erected to the right of wood doors. The occupants, obviously officers, have acquired camp chairs, and a hitching post for horses is visible. It appears they don't plan on any active campaigning in the foreseeable future. Comforts such as these were normally reserved for rear echelon and staff officer types.*

Above: *This image of Confederate winter quarters at Manassas, Virginia, illustrates the construction talents of men trying to survive a harsh Virginia winter. Small log buildings, some with shake roofs, have been laid out with proper streets. The structures were probably occupied by members of a "mess' who ate and lived together in relative harmony with small armies of lice.*

101

Above: *Commands were accompanied by specific drum beats or drum rolls whose meaning was immediately recognizable to the soldiers after endless hours of drill.*

Below: *Confederate musicians played instruments of prewar manufacture, such as the wood clarinet, copper bugle with brass garland and the plain maple shell drum. Wright and Bell, Confederate Drum Manufactory, furnished the painted drum of the 13th Virginia Infantry prior to February 1862.*

Members of Confederate bands were combatants. Bands in southern armies were not as prevalent as in the Union Army and were generally smaller. Musicians in gray made up no more than 125 bands during the war.

Regimental bands often consisted of a mixture of woodwind, brass and percussion instruments. Bandsmen played instruments for all manner of ceremonial occasions but during battle became stretcher-bearers and surgeon's assistants, transported and cared for the wounded, and buried the dead. Field musicians played an even more important role in military life. Fifers and drummers for infantry, and buglers for cavalry, announced the daily cadence of camp life, from roll call to taps. Even more critical, their drum rolls and bugle calls directed tactical movements on the battlefield where verbal orders could not be heard over the din of battle.[13]

Flags

The most easily recognized and revered relics of the war are the tattered flags of both sides, preserved in government, state and private repositories around the country. To this day no other object associated with the Civil War elicits so much emotion. Army regulations revised in 1861 stated that Union regiments would carry two silk flags, each about six feet square – the national flag and a regimental flag. Unit flags of different design and size were specified for infantry, artillery and cavalry. In addition there was a system of designating flags for brigade, division, corps and specialty services. The Quartermaster Department was responsible for procurement and issuance of colors and accomplished this through depots in Philadelphia, New York and Cincinnati. These depots secured flags through a host of independent contractors such as Tiffany & Company in New York, Horstmann Brothers in Philadelphia, Sisco Brothers in Baltimore, and John Shilleto in Cincinnati. As the war progressed many unit colors were painted with the names of engagements in which the units had fought. By 1865 some flags were covered with these battle honors.

There are many flags of strikingly different patterns associated with the Confederate States of America. In its four years of existence the country had three different national flags, and then there were at least half a dozen different battleflag patterns, silk presentation flags, state flags, garrison flags, naval flags, headquarters flags, signal flags and miniature personal flags. The Confederate flag most people recognize is the familiar red flag bearing the star-studded St. Andrew's Cross, the battleflag of the Army of Northern Virginia, but it was just one of many. The source of these flags was the Quartermaster Department with issuance through a depot system just as with the Federal Army, but the parallel ended there. Almost any available textile was used to construct flags, including wool, cotton and even silk from wedding dresses.

Many early Confederate flags were emblazoned with patriotic mottos such as "Victory or Death," "Defenders of Our Homes," or "Any Fate But Submission." Others carried the nicknames of the units that bore them, like "Dixie Rebels," "Cherokee Braves," or "Wakulla Guards."[14] Regardless of pattern or sentiment, each flag was the soul of the regiment to be protected at all cost. Federal troops made every effort to capture Confederate flags and the mortality rate among color bearers was proof of the intensity of such efforts. Even in defeat there is an elusive mystique about flags of the Confederacy that insures continued interest in them.

Above: *Besides the National Flag, Federal regiments carried a silk state regimental flag such as this Pennsylvania Infantry color. Confederate regiments carried only one flag, often a battle flag, silk early and wool bunting later, that sometimes displayed unit designation and battle honors.*

Left: *Confederate flags exhibited amazing diversity: that of the 1st and 3rd Florida had reversed colors on the St. Andrews cross.*

CHAPTER FIVE

War on the Water

"I would defy anyone in the world to tell when it is day or night if he is confined below without any way of marking time. If a person were blind folded and carried below and then turned loose he would imagine himself in a swamp."
(Sailor aboard the ironclad CSS *Atlanta*)

T HE UNITED STATES HAD built a strong merchant marine tradition in the northeast coastal areas during the first half of the nineteenth century. Whaling fleets of New England and commercial transports sailing from the ports of Boston, New York, Philadelphia and Baltimore were well established, and major shipyards flourished in these locations. There was also a strong naval tradition built on the victories of the Revolutionary War and the War of 1812, but government interest in maintaining and modernizing the Navy waned due to financial constraints and the policy of avoiding overseas commitments. Thus, the United States Navy began the war in 1861 with just ninety capital ships and other vessels, only forty-two of which were in active service[1], many in disrepair. They were manned by a total of 9,057 officers and enlisted men.[2] The United States Marine Corps was even less prepared with a complement of only 1,775 officers and men.[3]

Interestingly enough, it was a plan conceived by aging Commander-in-Chief of the Army, Major General Winfield Scott, and presented to President Abraham Lincoln that became the basis for the Union naval strategy. It was known as the Anaconda Plan, named after the huge snake that killed its prey by constriction, and was intended literally to strangle the South. The plan called for a blockade of southern ports from Virginia to Texas and the splitting of the Confederacy by the U.S. Navy gaining control of the

Mississippi River while the Army maintained pressure on Confederate land forces.[4] The plan looked fine on paper, but there were only two ships then available to guard the whole coast.

Secretary of the Navy Gideon Welles was tasked with implementing the naval aspect of the plan and proceeded to buy every vessel that would float and arm them with every gun that would shoot. He cobbled together a polyglot armada consisting of everything from first class frigates and screw steamers to converted tugs and ferryboats. The results were the North Atlantic Blockading Squadron, South Atlantic Blockading Squadron and West Gulf Squadron. These were to blockade 3,549 miles of coast with no fewer than 180 sites suitable for landings, the largest blockade ever attempted by any country.[5] In addition, there was the Mississippi River Squadron, the riverine Navy, in some cases crewed by Army troops, to force the dissection of the Confederacy. Welles realized that existing Navy ships and those civilian craft purchased and converted to naval use would be insufficient for the task, and he also knew that the fledgling Confederate Navy was hard at work building ironclad vessels to break the blockade.

Ironclads and tinclads

The backbone of all the Union fleets would be the conventional wood-hulled steam frigates, such as *Wabash* and *Minnesota*, and steam sloops like *Pensacola*, *Hartford*, *Brooklyn* and *Kearsarge* armed with large-bore Parrott rifles and Dahlgren guns. But to combat the Confederate armored threat Secretary Welles secured from Congress $1,500,000 to build three prototype ironclads.

Merrick and Sons of Philadelphia built the *New Ironsides*. The ship was commissioned in August 1862 and was a traditional broadside type ship, classed as a steam frigate. She was only partially armored – 170 feet of her 230-foot hull was covered with 4.5-inch iron plate. This belt covered the sides and the deck amidships, leaving the bow and stern unarmored. The main battery of this behemoth was sixteen 11-inch Dahlgren smoothbore cannon.[6] The ship served faithfully and well in a conventional role throughout the war and was the only ship of this type built

The USS *Galena* was the not-so-good idea of Cornelius S. Bushnell of Mystic, Connecticut. This ship was a small corvette covered with 3-inch iron plate. *Galena's* first real test came in May 1862 when she and other vessels steamed up the James River and engaged Fort Darling, seven miles below Richmond. She took 28 hits, of which 18 went right on through her armor, killing 13 and wounding 11 of her crew. That ended her days as an armored ship. The plate was removed and *Galena* spent the rest of her service as a wooden-hulled ship on blockade duty.[7]

Above: *The USS* Galena, *a corvette mounting only six guns and with three inches of armor, had her baptism of fire at Drewry's Bluff where the plunging fire of Ft. Darling's 8-inch Columbiads demolished the vessel. Marine John Mackie returned fire with a musket, rallied survivors of the riddled vessel and won the Medal of Honor.*

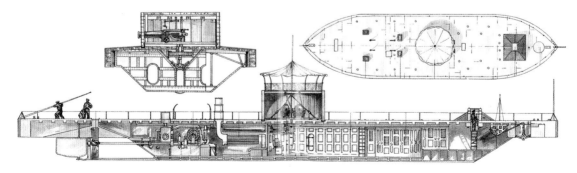

The third new design, USS *Monitor*, was the brainchild of the Swedish genius, John Ericcson. He was egocentric and already unpopular with Navy brass, and his design was a radical departure from current naval thinking. Nevertheless, Ericcson received a contract and built his ship at Green Point, Long Island. From start to finish it took just 100 days and cost $275,000.00. *Monitor* was a 172- by 41.5-foot armored raft supported by a 122- by 34-foot wooden hull below the water line, propelled by a steam-driven single screw.[8]

Her steam-powered revolving turret, 20 feet in diameter and weighing 120 tons, mounted two 11-inch smoothbore Dahlgren guns that could each fire a 165-pound solid shot every seven minutes to a range of one mile.[9] The propellant was 15 pounds of Du Pont's Mammoth powder. The vessel rode so low in the water that it was called a "tin can on a shingle," "cheesebox on a raft," and even "Ericcson's Folly." It was also a very small and difficult target.

Naval warfare was changed forever by the events of March 9, 1862, when *Monitor* and *Virginia* fought in Hampton Roads. Though the range was at times point blank, no projectile penetrated the armor of either ship and the battle was a tactical draw with no one killed in either crew. The age of wooden fighting ship was over. However, most importantly, the Union's blockade remained in effect and the last real opportunity of European intervention in the war faded away.[10]

Above: *The historic naval battle between ironclads* Monitor *and* Virginia. *The two 11-inch Dahlgrens in the turret of the smaller ship and the six 9-inch Dahlgren smoothbores, two 6.4-inch and two 7-inch Brooke rifles in the casemate of the behemoth pounded each other at close range, the heavy projectiles caroming harmlessly off the angled armor plate.*

Left: *The* Monitor *was a difficult target. Her decks were almost awash and an armored belt extended down below the waterline, so it was impossible to penetrate the hull or damage the propulsion unit. The turret always presented a curved surface that made any projectile strike a glancing blow at best, and the gun ports were shuttered or turned away except when the guns were run out to fire.*

The success of *Monitor* was startling and greatly changed naval thinking overnight. Additional monitor-class vessels were constructed with modifications and upgrades. *Tecumseh* was fitted with huge 15-inch Dahlgren guns that fired shot that weighed 400 pounds or more. Double-turreted versions like *Chickasaw*, *Winebago* and *Onondaga* were afloat in 1864. Regrettably, monitor-class vessels were not truly seaworthy and had a tendency to take on water during rough seas, so their use was restricted to coastal waters at best. Some were in commission in 1898 and still afloat in 1909.

Riverine warfare

Ships that served with the Mississippi Squadron on the restricted waterways of the interior faced different challenges. Limited maneuverability and danger from the shore line, sometimes close on both sides, dictated their armament. The Squadron's hybrid-type river monitors, such as *Osage*, were armored sternwheelers with a turret mounting two guns.[11] Other gunboats, like *Forest Rose*, were former civilian steamers, variously armed and armored, and called "tinclads." They were usually side- or stern-wheelers of light draft for use in shallow rivers, and more than sixty were eventually obtained. They had one-half to three-quarters of an inch thick iron armor along the lower

Below: The inland waterways dictated a different kind of fighting ship, one that could navigate shallow, twisting rivers with sand bars and snags, and the ever present danger of small arms fire and artillery from the bank which was often only a few feet away. Modified riverboats like Forest Rose, *a lightly armored stern wheeler, were the answer. This type vessel earned the name "tinclad" but it was sufficient protection for the task at hand.*

hulls and up as high as eleven feet on the superstructure. This armor was effective against small arms fire and light artillery but useless against heavy guns.[12] Their ordnance normally consisted of howitzers in the bow.

"Cotton clad" rams were another stop-gap effort developed by the Union for river warfare. Charles Rivers Ellet converted nine antiquated steamboats into rams by covering the bows on the boats with iron and protecting the boilers and superstructure

with cotton bales. These ships mounted no guns and their sole purpose was to ram enemy ships. This idea was executed under the patronage of Secretary of War Edwin M. Stanton, who gave Ellet an Army commission, just one example of the Army meddling in naval affairs that occurred all too frequently.[13]

The most powerful Federal vessel on inland waters was the huge *Choctaw*, a side-wheel steamboat that had been built in St. Louis and was converted into an ironclad fitted with an iron bow ram. She was a flat-bottom boat with a draft of only seven feet, amazing considering her size, with independently active sidewheels that facilitated turning in confined quarters. The vessel had three casemates, a large one forward and two smaller amidships. The forward position mounted three 9-inch smoothbores and one 100-pounder rifle. There were two 24-pounder howitzers in the second casemate, and two Parrott 30-pounder rifles in front of the wheels – a veritable floating fort.[14]

River warfare needed special craft, and Samuel M. Pook designed for the War Department, not the Navy Department, river ironclads known as City-class gunboats. They were also referred to as "Pook Turtles" and were specifically designed to fight on shallow inland waterways.[15] The contractor James B. Eads built four at the Carondelet Marine Ways outside St. Louis and three at the Marine Railway and Ship Yard at Mound City. Each vessel was 175 feet long and had a beam of 50 feet, and a flat bottom with a draft of only

Above: *USS* Choctaw *was one of the strangest looking vessels of the riverine force, a sort of naval Frankenstein. Her 9-inch smoothbores and 100-pounder rifle were more than adequate, but her two-knot speed against the current was not. This vessel was another example of making do with what was available at the time.* Choctaw *performed well during the second Vicksburg Campaign, and while under heavy fire was hit 53 times without sustaining appreciable damage.*

Right: *When USS* Cairo *was raised in 1964, and subsequently restored, one of the exciting discoveries was the method of sighting main armament in the dark casemate with only small battle lanterns for illumination. The guns had a wide white stripe painted down the top of the barrel. Sighting was as simple as "point and shoot."*

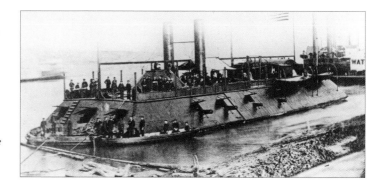

Below: *The sailors called the big 13-inch mortars "chowder pots" in jest but serving the big weapons was serious work. These schooners were sail-powered with all the masts, sails and rigging to manage. Before the mortar could go into action all overhead obstructions had to be cleared and carefully stowed.*

6 feet. It was powered by a paddle wheel driven by two coal-burning engines with five steam boilers. The whole hull was covered by an oblong, rectangular casemate with 2½ inch thick iron armor plate slopping 45 degrees in the front and 35 degrees on the sides.

Armament varied on different boats in the class. *Cairo* was armed with three 8-inch smoothbore guns forward, two 42-pounder rifles and two 32-pounder smoothbores on each side, and two 32-pounder smoothbores in the stern. She was manned by a crew of 175 officers and men.[16] *Carondelet* was the first City-class vessel launched, in October 1861, followed by *Louisville*, *St. Louis*, *Cairo*, *Cincinnati* and *Mound City*. The *Cairo* found her place in history in 1862 when she was sunk by a Confederate torpedo or mine in the Yazoo River. She was raised in 1964, and is one of the very few surviving ships of the Civil War.

Mortar Squadron
Mortar sloops and mortarscows were other special purpose designs. In November 1861 Secretary Welles authorized then Commander David Dixon

Porter to form a Mortar Squadron using common schooners specially reinforced and mounting huge 13 inch mortars. Welles's purpose was to reduce the Confederate forts below New Orleans.[17] The 13-inch mortar, Model 1861, was mounted on a Navy mortar circle made of wood set on eccentric rollers that were engaged by four levers for traverse or disengaged to let the platform rest on solid support during firing.[18] Flag Officer Andrew Hull Foote used the same type of mortars mounted on lightly armored barges, mortarscows, that were towed into position for bombardments. These mortars fired a 220-pound explosive shell over 4,000 yards and were very demoralizing and effective.

Ship armament

Civil War ships, whether ocean-going, coastal or inland water types, relied more and more on large, heavy-caliber rifles and smoothbores. Parrott made a variety of guns for the Navy. The distinct configuration of the banded breech was the same as on the smaller Army field and siege and garrison models, but some of the naval guns were very large indeed.[19] The 4.2-inch 30-pounder weighed 3,350 pounds – and it was the little one! There were a 5.3-inch 60-pounder, a 6.4-inch 100pounder, an 8-inch 200-pounder, and the largest, a 10-inch 300-pounder, that weighed some 27,000 pounds and had a range of over 4,000 yards. Navy Parrotts, the larger rifles, seemed to have an even greater propensity to burst at the muzzle during firing than Army models and not unsurprisingly were not held in great esteem by crews.

The other pieces that saw extensive service with the Federal Navy in many calibers were the various Dahlgren guns, from the little bronze 12-pounder howitzer on an assault carriage to the enormous 15-inch shell guns used in later

Above: *Model 1861 6.4-inch or 100-pounder Parrott Rifle on field-expedient barbette carriage that allows the barrel to elevate but not traverse.*

Below: *Full gun crew supervised by an officer and assisted by a Marine practice with a 9-inch Dalhgren smoothbore gun mounted on a pivot carriage aboard USS* Mendota *in 1864.*

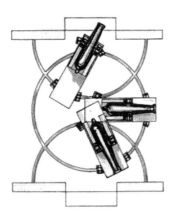

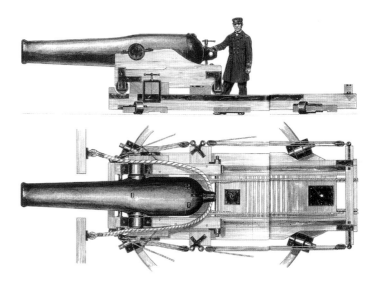

Above and right: *The inboard pivot mount provided the maximum flexibility for use of the gun. The gun truck traveled on iron track affixed to the deck, allowing the gun to swivel 360 degrees. The armament could go into action either to port or starboard with equal ease. Even though an 11-inch Dahlgren gun weighed 16,000 pounds it could be traversed smoothly on this pivot mount. Recoil was absorbed, moving to the rear of the carriage. The gun was brought back into battery by a system of block and tackle on either side of the piece.*

monitor-class ship turrets. These each weighed about 42,000 pounds and fired a solid shot weighing 440 pounds, a real armor-crusher. The 9- and 11-inch Dahlgren guns were the most popular and it was an 11-inch pivot gun on the USS *Kearsarge* that inflicted the mortal blows to the Confederate raider *Alabama* in the English Channel in June 1864.[20]

Different types of carriages were used as placement on vessels dictated. Rifles and shell guns used as bow guns or stern chasers were mounted on pivot carriages which allowed maximum traverse aboard ship whether on deck or within a casemate. A well-manned, long-range gun with the flexibility allowed by this mount was a very effective weapon. A wooden Navy four-wheel truck or Marsilly carriage was normally used for those guns that were utilized in broadside positions. Navy guns mounted ashore used the same front and center pintle carriages as the Army's siege and garrison pieces.[21]

The new steel navies led to the development of "armor-punching," steel-nosed, chilled shot that not only penetrated armor but started bolts and caused lethal fragmentation and splinters inside the confined areas of the target ship. Smoothbore rounds were called cored shot, while a projectile for a rifle was termed either a shot or bolt.

The Confederate Navy

The Confederate Navy did not even exist when the war began. There were the hastily formed state navies of North Carolina, South Carolina, Louisiana and several others, but no ships of any consequence. What did lie in the southern states were extant naval bases and ports with their dockyards and facilities, vast naval stores and cannon foundries. Confederate state authorities moved immediately to seize all of these sites.

The Gosport Navy Yard at Norfolk, Virginia, provided the greatest ordnance windfall of over 1,198 heavy guns, including almost 1,000 32-pounders and over 50 fine 9-inch Dahlgren guns, along with tons of powder and projectiles.[22] Seizure of Pensacola, Charleston and Mobile provided additional supplies. Luckily for the Confederates, the Tredegar Foundry and Bellona Foundry at Richmond, existing cannon foundries, were in Virginia. The Confederate Navy was also blessed with a cadre of veteran officers, with over 350 former Union Navy men joining their ranks.[23] Regardless of these fortuitous circumstances, however, the Union possessed almost total command of the seas from the outset.

Confederate Secretary of the Navy Stephen R. Mallory arrived in Richmond on June 3, 1861, to develop plans for mobilizing a navy. He had always been a quiet patron of ironclads and torpedoes and proceeded immediately to include these unconventional ideas in his planning. Mallory knew his resources were limited and realized he could build only a small navy and thus gambled on revolutionary naval strategy and futuristic weapons to offset the overwhelming strength in numbers of the Union Navy.[24]

The Confederate Navy selected three courses of action against the Union Navy and its blockade. Ironclads would be built to neutralize the Union fleets and break the blockade. Fast commerce raiders would be acquired overseas and unleashed to disrupt Federal maritime trading activities. Lastly, the Rebels would develop and exploit unconditional methods of warfare in the form of submarines, torpedo boats and mines to confound and demoralize the Union Navy.

Lieutenant John M. Brooke convinced Mallory that the Confederacy could build her own ironclads. Brooke proceeded with plans to raise the *Merrimac*, a Union wooden frigate that had been scuttled and burned to the water line at the Gosport Navy Yard, and rebuild her using the hull and engines with an armored superstructure. The result was the CSS *Virginia*, the first Confederate ironclad, launched in February 1862 and the model for others to follow.[25]

The design was chosen because of its simplicity and ease of fabrication. The casemate was fabricated of wood, two feet thick, covered with four inches of laminated iron plate. The ship was armed with ten guns: six 9-inch Dahlgrens and two 6.4-inch rifles, plus two 7-inch rifles of Brooke's design. These big Brooke rifles were mounted one in each end of the casemate, on pivot carriages that allowed them to fire along the vessel's centerline or from port or starboard quarter ports. The other eight guns were mounted in broadside, four to each side, and the submerged bow was fitted with a 1,500-pound cast iron ram three feet below the water line.

Virginia was impressive and formidable, but she had a deep draft of 23 feet, was very difficult to maneuver, and slow. Several other ironclads were transformed from other types of vessels but the best were those built new from the keel up. *Arkansas, Georgia, Louisiana,*

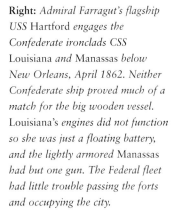

Right: *Admiral Farragut's flagship* USS Hartford *engages the Confederate ironclads CSS* Louisiana *and* Manassas *below New Orleans, April 1862. Neither Confederate ship proved much of a match for the big wooden vessel.* Louisiana's *engines did not function so she was just a floating battery, and the lightly armored* Manassas *had but one gun. The Federal fleet had little trouble passing the forts and occupying the city.*

Mississippi and *Tennessee* all followed the same basic pattern, of large dimensions with a casemate mounting ten or more heavy guns. Designed to carry 22 guns, *Mississippi* was 264 feet long with a beam of 62 feet and a draft of 7 feet. By contrast *Tennessee* and *Arkansas* were only 165 feet long with a beam of 35 feet.[26]

By Spring 1862 an effort was made to standardize design and increase speed and maneuverability. The result was the smaller Richmond-class ironclad. Other classes followed but all were based on the casemate model. Improvements were made throughout construction, but all Confederate ironclads were plagued with underpowered engines. Speed and maneuverability were never achieved. Some could hardly go up-stream against an outgoing tide. Some were destroyed before completion because of the proximity of capture.

Commerce raiders from England

In 1861 Secretary Mallory dispatched agents to England with one million dollars to acquire fast, lightly armed commerce raiders. He knew such ships would wreak havoc on commerce and force the Union Navy to withdraw ships from the blockade to chase them. While some early raiders like *Sumter* were converted steamers, the most successful were built in England using modified Royal Navy gunboat plans.

The *Florida* and *Alabama* became legends. Both had steam propulsion engines with full sailing rigs and propellers that could be raised when under sail. They were constructed of wood, allowing

Above: *William C. Miller & Sons of Liverpool built CSS* Florida. *The ship was 184 feet 6 inches x 27 feet 2 inches x 14 feet and designed to mount eight guns. The wooden-hulled ship was steam- and sail-powered with a lifting screw that could be raised to extend cruising range. During her highly successful two-year cruise she took thirty-seven prizes, one of which was the* Jacob Bell *shown here being chased and about to be captured and burned. The* Florida *was illegally seized by USS* Wachusetts *at Bahia Bay, Brazil, and taken to Philadelphia to Prize Court where the judge ordered her returned to Confederate authorities. Subsequently, she was taken down to Hampton Roads but prior to reverting to Confederate control CSS* Florida *mysteriously sank.*

Right: *John Laird, Sons and Company built* CSS Alabama *under contract for Commander James Dunwoody Bulloch, one of the more successful Confederate procurement agents.* Alabama *was commanded by Captain Raphael Semmes and enjoyed a career even more successful than* Florida. *During her rampage* Alabama *destroyed USS* Hatteras, *the only Federal warship sunk on the high seas by a Confederate cruiser. The* Alabama *was eventually sunk off Cherbourg, France, by* USS Kearsarge *on June 19, 1864. Semmes escaped and returned to the Confederacy in January 1865. French divers located the grave of the* Alabama *in the 1990s and some artifacts have been recovered.*

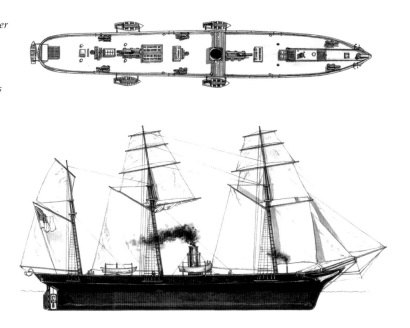

repair in the most primitive ports when necessary, and were armed with the most modern English rifles and guns. What these ships couldn't outrun, they could outshoot. *Alabama* was 210 feet long by 32 feet, manned by a crew of 145 officers and men, cruised at a speed of 13 knots, and mounted eight guns, six 32-pounder smoothbores in broadside, one 68-pounder smoothbore on pivot amidships, and a 6.4-inch 100-pounder Blakely rifle on pivot just forward of the smoke stack.[27]

The *Alabama* alone captured or destroyed sixty-nine Federal commercial ships valued at $7,000,000 during her 22-month career. Commerce raiders destroyed some five percent of the Union merchant fleet, and for every vessel destroyed the Union fleet lost eight others to exorbitant insurance rates and transfer to other flags to avoid the conflict.[28] Claims resulting from activities of these commerce raiders were being settled for years after the war was over.

Submarines

Another effort to break the blockade by the Confederates was made with undersea craft. Submarines and semi-submersibles were not a new idea but no operational craft had yet been developed. Baxter Watson and James McClintock, partners in a New Orleans machine shop, and Horace Lawton Hunley, a lawyer with plenty of money, built the submarine *Pioneer* in New Orleans in the winter of 1861-1862. It was a 20-foot long craft with a hand-cranked screw and manned by a crew of two. However, she was scuttled to avoid capture by Union forces when the city was occupied that spring. A second boat, *Pioneer II* or *American Diver*, was built at Mobile but was lost in rough seas near Fort Morgan while attempting to attack a blockader.

The Singer Secret Service Corps, a clandestine group interested in mining harbors and railroad sabotage, financed and constructed the third and unnamed craft in Mobile during the summer of 1863. They sent her by rail to Charleston for operational testing.[29] The submarine was 40 feet long overall with a claustrophobic crew space, originally an old boiler, about 25 feet long and just 4 feet high and $3\frac{1}{2}$ feet wide. She had a keel ballast release system in case of a need for emergency surfacing, and ballast tanks forward and aft that could be pumped out to increase buoyancy. Twin snorkel pipes with a bellows for air intake when near the surface were mounted behind the forward hatch, which also housed the captain's navigational viewing port. The captain/pilot steered and operated the diving planes to

Below: The submarine C. L. Hunley, relegated to obscurity after the Civil War, has become a hot historical property in the last decade. Clive Cussler, the adventure writer, became interested in the story and found the resting place of the boat only about 1,000 feet from where she sank USS Housatonic. Hollywood made a decent movie about the exploits of the submarine several years ago, and stories have appeared in several magazines including National Geographic, whose website has a 3-D interactive view of the Hunley. Patriotic organizations have given the remains of some of the crew found inside proper burial. Current plans call for the submarine to be the centerpiece of a new maritime museum in Charleston.

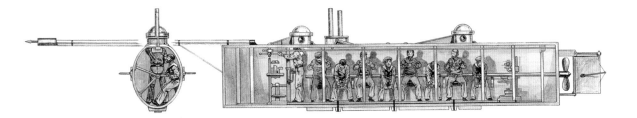

regulate direction and depth, while eight crewmen sat side by side in the cold, dark crew compartment, manipulating a hand cranked propeller that pushed the boat through the water.

Brave and dedicated crewmen training in the strange craft once sat on the ocean bottom for 2½ hours in pitch dark because their only light, a candle, ceased to burn after just twenty-five minutes due to oxygen deprivation. Two disastrous training dives resulted in the loss of two crews, including Mr. Hunley. After his death the craft was named in his honor. The submarine *C. L. Hunley* made naval history on the evening of February 14, 1864, when she sank USS *Housatonic* off Charleston using a barbed spar torpedo/mine filled with 135 pounds of powder. The submarine was lost in the same action, but was found in 1995 and recovered in 2002.[30]

The David torpedo-boats

The Southern Torpedo Company of Charleston built a number of semi-submersible torpedo boats in 1863. These cigar-shaped craft were 50 feet long, had a crew of four, and were powered by steam engines capable driving the boats to seven knots. Each was fitted with a spar torpedo filled with 100 pounds of black powder. The craft was named the *David*, an allusion to the David and Goliath biblical story. David-class boats made at least three attempts to break the blockade

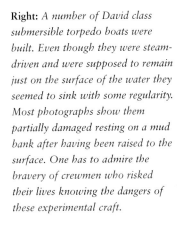

Right: *A number of David class submersible torpedo boats were built. Even though they were steam-driven and were supposed to remain just on the surface of the water they seemed to sink with some regularity. Most photographs show them partially damaged resting on a mud bank after having been raised to the surface. One has to admire the bravery of crewmen who risked their lives knowing the dangers of these experimental craft.*

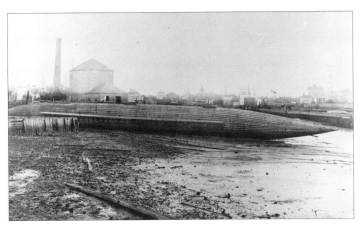

in Charleston harbor and achieved some success against *New Ironsides*, which was badly damaged.[31] Construction of other David-class boats was started in Savannah and Wilmington and near Houston, but accidents and the end of the war precluded completion.

The Confederate Navy was certainly more active in the submarine field but the U.S. Navy Department did authorize Martin Thomas of Philadelphia to build a submarine craft in November 1861. This was the *Alligator*, a 45-foot long vessel that proved utterly useless and was lost under tow on April 2, 1863, on the way to Charleston.[32]

Torpedo-mines

What were called torpedoes during the war, and are the modern day marine mine, were also known as "infernal machines" by naval men of the 19th century. Use of these devices may well have been roundly criticized, but their deployment proved to be a very effective defensive and offensive measure for harbors and rivers. Mathew Fontaine Maury is known as the "Father of Mine Warfare." Famous former head of the U.S. Naval Observatory, he left the Federal Navy when Virginia seceded from the Union in the spring of 1861, and became commander of the Confederate Torpedo Bureau in Richmond.

Most torpedo-mine designs were of the "keg" or "frame" type and were very simple contraptions. Water-tight containers were filled with a substantial amount of black powder and either fitted with a contact fuze or wire attached to a galvanic battery ashore that allowed detonation by an observant operator. Some containers were no more than glass demi-johns, while others were copper cylinders. There were also stake torpedoes that looked like

Above: *This copper powder container was just one of a variety of very successful Confederate floating mines encountered in coastal waters. Federal naval personnel were constantly alert for such devices.*

Below: *Recovered mines had to be very carefully disarmed by qualified personnel. Many professional military men considered any kind of mine warfare barbaric and would have nothing to do with it.*

artillery projectiles, with contact fuzes mounted on pilings just below the water's surface.

There is no question but that these weapons were effective. Their psychological effect was noted as "torpedo fever" and large numbers of Federal men were diverted from other duties to clear mines and build booms and sweeps to protect Union ships. Seven ironclads and twenty-two wooden gunboats were sent to the bottom by mines in what was the birth of a new kind of warfare.[33]

The blockade runners

Blockade running was a necessary feature of the Confederacy's war because of the need for vast amounts of supplies of all kinds, military and domestic, from overseas markets. As this trade developed, cargoes were sent out in "neutral" vessels from England and other European countries to Bermuda, Nassau and Cuba. There, the cargoes were unloaded, stored in Confederate-leased warehouses and sent on to the Confederacy as transportation permitted in fast, sleek "runners." These vessels would bring in contraband cargoes of munitions, medicines, hides, food, even pins, needles and tools and take out bales of cotton to be transported back to Europe. Wilmington, Charleston and Savannah on the Atlantic coast and

Right: *The successful blockade runner* Hornet. *Captains and crew of most blockade runners were civilians. Some were even English officers on leave of absence. The trade was very lucrative and many high government officers owned silent partnerships in blockade running companies. Fortunes were made on just one successful venture. Up until mid-1863 business was very good but the Union Navy slowly tightened the noose. The majority of runners were captured or run aground by the end of 1864.*

Mobile, New Orleans and Galveston on the Gulf coast were all active ports for as long as they remained open. Wilmington was the last to close, on January 15, 1865, with the fall of Ft. Fisher.

Ships used in this dangerous but lucrative business included those that were unarmed, fast, shallow draft vessels of large cargo capacity, with side paddlewheels and iron hulls. Quite a few were Clyde River steamers converted to this purpose. As the blockade became more stringent, vessels appeared with hinged masts, telescoping smokestacks and camouflage paint schemes. Maneuverability and speeds of 12 and 13 knots were necessary if the vessel were to successfully run the Union gauntlet. The *R.E. Lee* and *Hornet* both boasted the rakish lines and low silhouette of the typical runner.[34]

The Brooke rifles

John Mercer Brooke, a former United States Navy officer who resigned his commission to join the Virginia State Navy at the first hostilities and shortly thereafter the Confederate Navy, developed the Confederate answer to the heavy Parrott rifle. A genius, he worked on plans for his gun and, as peviously mentioned, the conversion of the *Merrimac* into the ironclad *Virginia*. He became Chief of the Bureau of Ordnance and Hydrography in March 1863, which post he

Below: *A double-banded Brooke rifle that was captured by Federal troops is being hauled off to some collection point under a captured Confederate sling cart. These wheels of the cart are 10 feet in diameter. This was the manner in which these huge rifles had to be moved because of their immense weight. An excellent group of Brooke rifles, including many rare variations, may be seen at the Washington Navy Yard, and there are several in the Charleston, S.C., area.*

Right: *A 6.4-inch Read shell for a 100-pounder rifle. The threaded fuze is missing but it was some type of brass percussion fuze. The shell has a copper sabot that took the rifling of the barrel to impart spin. The unfinished body of the shell has bourrelets, or bearing surfaces. Only these surfaces were machined, to speed manufacture.*

Far right: *A 6.4-inch Brooke bolt for a 100-pounder rifle. This is an armor puncher for use against ironclads. The body of the shell shows distinct bourrelets that are typical of many Confederate projectiles. This round also has a copper sabot, which is quite common with Confederate ordnance.*

held until the end of the war.

The Brooke gun was produced at Tredegar Foundry in Richmond in 1861 and the Confederate Naval Ordnance Works at Selma, Alabama, by 1863. Like the Parrott, the Brooke was a cast iron tube with a two inch thick wrought iron reinforcing band at the breech, although the Brooke was of heavier construction with a sharper taper to the barrel. Brooke tubes have been noted single-, double- and even triple-banded. Unlike the Parrott, which had a solid reinforce, the Brooke had several rings, each about six inches wide. The rifling was the "hook-slant" type used in the English Blakely rifle. Brooke rifles were made in 6.4-inch, 7-inch, 8-inch and 11-inch calibers. Smoothbores were made in 10- and 11-inch configuration.

The Brooke was unquestionably the most powerful gun in the Confederate arsenal. The 10-inch smoothbore weighed around 22,000 pounds and fired a wrought iron ball with very heavy charges. Against Federal ironclads it was terribly effective at short range. A triple-banded Brooke using a charge of 16 pounds of powder fired a 140-pound wrought iron bolt through 8 inches of iron and 18 inches of wood at 260 yards.[35] The smaller 6.4-inch and 7-inch Brookes had a range of four miles and weighed about 14,000 pounds. One-third of them went on board Confederate vessels. Working night and day, it took between two-and-a-half and three months to manufacture a 7-inch Brooke. Selma produced no fewer

Left: *Marines and Navy personnel from the North Atlantic Blockading Squadron are rowed away from their ships on the disastrous combined services amphibious assault on Ft. Fisher in January 1865. It was not an auspicious beginning for the Marines' effort to redefine their role in the military establishment. Nevertheless, the potential of a specially trained and highly motivated elite force was attractive to some visionaries and it was obvious that inter-service cooperation was going to be a necessity in the future.*

than 102 Brookes of various caliber and Tredegar produced at least another 62 of various calibers.[36]

The Confederate Navy was unable to combat the effectiveness of the Union blockade, and was too weak and too ineffective to influence the outcome of the war. It did manage to build technologically advanced warships and put more than 130 of them into service during the war along with other new weapons systems, but never had the resources to seriously challenge the Federal Navy. Both navies developed sea craft and weapons systems that changed the course of naval warfare forever.

The Civil War was also the turning point in the mission of marines, both North and South. Before the war, marines had been used as boarding parties or to repel boarders and to man the fighting tops, stationing themselves aloft to fire down on officers and gun crews of the opposing vessels. With the advent of steam-driven ships and casemated vessels, this function became obsolete. There were no more tops to fight in, and boarding an ironclad was pointless since the opposing crew were protected behind armor and the boarders became subject to immediate decimation by large guns. Marines had to re-invent a reason for their existence, and they became a mobile strike force, ready instantly for any emergency.

Endnotes

CHAPTER ONE

l. Langellier, John P., *Army Blue, The Uniform of Uncle Sam's Regulars, 1848-1873*. Atglen, PA. Schiffer Military History, pgs. 288-321.
2. Ibid, p. 105.
3. Ibid, p. 109.
4. Farwell, Byron, *Encyclopedia of Nineteenth-Century Land Warfare*. New York, W. W. Norton & Co., p. 390.
5. Langellier, op. cit., p. 73.
6. Ibid, p. 141.
7. Ibid, p. 118.
8. Farwell, op. cit. pgs. 698-699.
9. Delano, Marfe Ferguson, and Mallen, Barbara C., *Echoes of Glory: Arms and Equipment of the Union*. Alexandria, VA. Time-Life Books, pgs. 168-169.
10. Ibid, p. 90.
11. Ibid, p. 125.
12. Langellier, op. cit. p. 189.
13. Langellier, op.cit. p. 288.
14. Langellier, op. cit. pgs. 94-95.
15. Langellier, op. cit. p.122 and 137.
16. Langellier, op. cit. pgs. 159-160.
17. McAfee, Michael J., and Langellier, John P., *Billy Yank, The Uniform of the Union Army, 1861-1865*, pgs. 28-36.
18. Langellier, op. cit. pgs. 170-171.
19. Delano and Mallen. op. cit. pgs.136-140.
20. Ibid, pgs.130-147.
21. Langellier, op. cit. p. 130.
22. Ibid, p. 320.
23. Ibid, p. 106.
24. Ibid, p. 293.
25. Delano and Mallen, op. cit. p. 115.
26. Ibid, p. 163.
27. Ibid, p. 165.
28. Ibid, p. 166.
29. Ibid, p. 169.
30. Langellier, op. cit. p. 115.
31. Ibid, p. 313.
32. Ibid, p. 313.

33. Delano and Mallen, op. cit. pgs. 164, 166.
34. Ibid, p. 192.
35. Ibid, pgs. 190-191.
36. Ibid, p. 190.
37. Langellier, op. cit. pgs. 315-316.
38. Delano and Mallen, op. cit. p. 169.
39. Langellier, op. cit. pgs. 171-172.
40. Ibid, p. 319.
41. Davis, William C., *Commanders of the Civil War*, London, Salamander Books, p. 138.
42. Delano, Marfe Ferguson, and Mallen, Barbara C., *Echoes of Glory, Arms and Equipment of the Confederacy*, Alexandria, VA, Time-Life Books, pgs. 81-82.
43. _____, *A Catalogue of Uniforms in the Collection of the Museum of the Confederacy*, Richmond, VA, Carter Printing Co., p. 8.
44. Ibid, p. 8.
45. Delano and Mallen, op. cit. pgs. 164-165.
46. *Catalogue of Uniforms*, p. 3.
47. Ibid, p. 122.
48. Delano and Mallen, op. cit. p. 118.
49. Ibid, p. 139.
50. Ibid, pgs. 150-151.
51. Ibid, pgs. 151-153.
52. Ibid, pgs. 154-155.
53. Ibid, pgs. 173-175.
54. Ibid, pgs. 95, 166-167.
55. Tice, Warren K., *Uniform Buttons of the United States, 1776-1865*, pgs. 196-242.

CHAPTER TWO

1. Reilly, Robert M., *United States Military Small Arms, 1816-1865*, Highland Park, NJ, The Gun Room Press, p. XVII.
2. Ibid, p. 4.
3. Ibid, p. 2.
4. Edwards, William B., *Civil War Guns*, Harrisburg, PA, The

Stackpole Company.
5. Reilly, op. cit. p. 75.
6. Ibid, p. 20.
7. Delano, Marfe Ferguson and Mallen, Barbara C., *Echoes of Glory: Arms and Equipment of the Union*, Alexandria, VA Time-Life Books, p. 24.
8. Reilly, op. cit. p. 1.
9. Edwards, op. cit. p. 77.
10. Ibid, p. 77.
11. Reilly, op. cit. pgs. 33-37.
12. Ibid, p. 65.
13. Ibid, p. 47.
14. Ibid, p. 45.
15. Delano and Mallen, op. cit. p. 53.
16. McAulay, John D., *Carbines of the Civil War, 1861-1865*, pgs. 9-12.
17. Ibid, pgs. 22-24.
18. Ibid, pgs. 25, 29.
19. Ibid, pgs. 37-38.
20. Ibid, pgs. 42-44.
21. Delano and Mallen, op. cit. p. 64.
22. McAulay, John D., *Civil War Pistols of the Union*, Lincoln, RI, Andrew Mowbray, Inc. p. 37.
23. Riley, op. cit. p. 209.
24. McAulay, op. cit. pgs. 70-71.
25. Ibid, pgs. 146-147.
26. Ibid, pgs. 157-160.
27. Ibid, pgs. 129-130.
28. Bezdek, Richard H., *American Swords and Sword Makers*, Boulder, CO, Paladin Press.
29. Thillmann, John H., *Civil War Cavalry & Artillery Sabers*, Lincoln, RI, Andrew Mowbray Publishers, p. 13.
30. Langellier, John P., *Army Blue, The Uniform of Uncle Sam's Regulars, 1848-1873*, Atglan, PA,Schiffer Publishing, Ltd., p. 291.
31. Delano and Mallen, op. cit. pgs. 202-203.
32. Ibid, pgs. 202,204.
33. Johnson, Paul D., *Civil War Cartridge Boxes of the Union*

Infantryman, Lincoln, RI, Andrew Mowbray Publishers, p. 292.
34. Ibid, p.327.
35. Delano and Mallen, op. cit. 204-205.
36. Sylvia, Stephen W., and O'Donnell, Michael J. *Civil War Canteens*, Orange, VA, Moss Publications, p.72.
37. Delano and Mallen, op. cit. pgs. 212 –213.
38. Ibid, p. 214.
39. Ibid, p. 217.
40. Noe, David, Yantz, Larry W., and Whisker, James B., *Firearms from Europe*, Rochester, NY, Rowe Publications, pgs.154-158.
41. Delano and Mallen, op. cit. P. 36.
42. Curtis, Chris C., *Systeme Lefaucheux*, Santa Ana, CA, Armslore Press, p.126.
43. Madaus, Howard Michael, *Small Arms Deliveries through Wilmington, NC in 1863.*, The Bulletin of the American Society of Arms Collectors, Spring 2002.
44. Huse, Caleb, *The Supplies for the Confederate Army*, Boston, MA, Press of T. R. Marvin, p.26.
45. Albaugh, William A., Benet, Hugh, Jr., and Simmons, Edward N., *Confederate Handguns*, Philadelphia, PA, Riling and Lentz, p. 129.
46. Forgett, Valmore J., and Serpette, Alain F. & Marie-Antoinette, *LeMat, The Man, The Gun*, Ridgefield, NJ, Navy Arms Co. p. 74.
47. Davies, Paul J., *C.S. Armory Richmond*, Carlisle, PA, Paul J. Davies, pgs. 349,351.
48. Murphy, John M. and Madaus, Howard Michael, *Confederate Rifles and Muskets*, Newport Beach, CA, Graphic Publishers, p. 219.
49. Ibid. p. 158.
50. Ibid. p. 136.
51. Albaugh, William A.,

Confederate Edged Weapons, New York, NY, Harper & Brothers, pgs. 98-100.
52. Ibid, p. 47.
53. Davies, op.cit. p. 17.
54. Sylvia and O'Donnell, op. cit. 8.

CHAPTER THREE
1. Stone, George Cameron, *A Glossary of the Construction, Decoration and Use of Arms and Armory*, New York, Jack Brussel, Publisher, p. 75.
2. Ripley, Warren, *Artillery and Ammunition of the Civil War*, New York, Van Nostrand Reinhold Company, p. 15.
3. Farwell, Byron, *The Encyclopedia of Nineteenth-Century Land Warfare*, New York, W. W. Norton & Co., p. 702.
4. Ripley, op. cit. p. 109.
5. Ibid, pgs. 26-27.
6. Dutton, William S., Du Pont, *One Hundred and Forty Years*, New York, Charles Scribner's Sons, pgs. 88-90.
7. Daniel, Larry J., and Gunter, Riley W., *Confederate Cannon Foundries*, Union City, TN, Pioneer Press, p. IV.
8. Delano, Marfe Ferguson, and Mallen, Barbara C., *Echoes of Glory, Arms and Equipment of the Union*, Alexandria, VA., Time-Life Books, p. 302.
9. Daniel, Larry J., *Cannoneers in Gray*, Univ. Alabama, p. 13.
10. Ripley, op. cit. p. 228.
11. Ibid, pgs. 18-19.
12. Ibid, p. 162.
13. Alexander, E. P., *Confederate Artillery Service*, Southern Historical Society papers, Vol. XI, p. 107.
14. Ripley, op.cit. p. 163.
15. Ibid, p. 109.
16. Delano and Mallen, op. cit. p. 300.
17. Ripley, op. cit., p. 300.
18. Ibid, pgs. 167-168.
19. Katcher, Philip, and Bryan, Tony, *American Civil War Artillery, 1861-1865 (1) Field Artillery*,

Oxford, UK, Osprey Publishing, p. 39.
20. Ripley, op. cit. pgs. 142-145, 341.
21. Ibid, p. 59.
22. Daniel and Gunter, op. cit. pgs. 97-99.
23. Ripley, op. cit. p. 228.
24. Ibid, p. 200.
25. Ibid, p. 114.
26. Ibid, p. 80.
27. Ibid, p. 30.
28. Ibid, pgs. 65-66.
29. Ibid, p. 146.
30. Ibid, .pgs.155-156.
31. Payne Ledgers, Library of the Museum of the Confederacy, Richmond, VA.
32. Bermuda Library, *Bermuda Royal Gazette*, October 31, 1865, Auction Notice.
33. Davis, William C., *The Illustrated Encyclopedia of the Civil War*, London, Salamander Books, Ltd., pgs. 280-281.
34. Faust, Patricia F., Editor, *Encyclopedia of the Civil War*, New York, Harper & Row, Publishers, p. 302.
35. Fuller, Claud E., *The Rifled Musket*, Harrisburg, PA., The Stackpole Company, pgs. 263-269.
36. Stelma, Tom, *Rapid Fire Guns of the Civil War, North South Trader's Civil War*, Vol. 29, No. 1, Orange, VA., Good Printers, Inc., pgs. 41-42.
37. Ibid, pgs. 39-41.
38. Ibid, pgs. 42-43.
39. Davis, William C., *Battlefields of the Civil War*, London, Salamander Books Ltd., pgs. 60-61.
40. Stelma, op. cit. pgs. 46-47.
41. Faust, op. cit. p. 830.

CHAPTER FOUR
1. Miller, F. T., ed. *The Photographic History of the Civil War*, Edison, NJ, The Blue & Gray Press, Vol. 4, p. 314.
2. Langellier, John P., *Army Blue, The Uniform of Uncle Sam's Regulars, 1848-1873*, Atglen, PA, Schiffer Military History,

pgs. 171-172.
3. Miller, op. cit. Vol. 4, p. 318.
4. Ibid, Vol. 4, p 368.
5. Davis, Burke, *The Civil War, Strange and Fascinating Facts*, New York, Wings Books, pgs. 51-52.
6. Miller, op.cit. Vol. 4, pgs. 370-375.
7. Davis, Burke, op. cit. p. 32.
8. Davis, Burke, op cit. p. 55.
9. Davis, William C., *Fighting Men of the Civil War*, London, Salamander Books Ltd., pgs. 226-227.
10. Dickey, Thomas S., and George, Peter C., *Field Artillery Projectiles of the American Civil War*, revised and supplemented 1993, Mechanicsville, VA, Arsenal Publishers II, p. 493.
11. Delano, Marfe Ferguson, and Delano, Barbara C., *Echoes of Glory, Arms and Equipment of the Union*, Alexandria, VA, Time-Life Books, p. 214.
12. Davis, William C., op. cit. p. 134.
13. Garofalo, Robert, and Elrod, Mark, *A Pictorial History of Civil War Era Musical Instruments & Military Bands*, Charlestown, West Virginia, Pictorial Histories Publishing Co. pgs. 53-57.
14. _____, *Colours of the Gray*, Richmond, Virginia, The Museum of the Confederacy, pgs. 6-7.

CHAPTER FIVE
1. Hearn, Chester G., *Naval Battles of the Civil War*, London, Salamander Books Ltd., p. 7.
2. McAulay, John D., *Civil War Small Arms of the U.S. Navy and Marine Corps*, Lincoln, Rhode Island, Andrew Mowbray Publishers, p. 59.
3. Donnelly, Ralph W., *The Confederate States Marine Corps*, Shippensburg, PA, White Mane Publishing Co., p. 1.
4. Warner, Ezra J., *General in Blue*, Baton Rouge, LA, Louisiana State University Press, p. 430

5. Faust, Patricia L., ed., *Illustrated Encyclopedia of the Civil War*, New York, Harper & Row, Publishers, p. 67.
6. Ibid, p. 525.
7. Ibid, p. 296.
8. Ibid, p. 504.
9. Hearn, op. cit. pgs. 28-29.
10. McAulay, op. cit. p. 83.
11. Ibid, p. 103.
12. Faust, op cit. p. 757.
13. Hearn, op. cit. pgs. 110-111.
14. Miller, F. T. ed., *The Photographic History of the Civil War*, Edison, NJ, The Blue & Gray Press, Vol. 3, pgs. 206-207.
15. Faust, op cit. p. 114.
16. Jones, Virgil Carrington, *The Story of a Civil War Gunboat, USS Cairo*, Washington, DC, National Park Service, pgs 8-18.
17. McAulay, op. cit. p. 85.
18. Ripley, Warren, *Artillery and Ammunition of the Civil War*, New York, Van Nostrand Reinhold Company, p. 220.
19. Ibid, pgs. 91-99.
20. Ibid, pgs. 97-101.
21. Ibid, pgs. 216-218.
22. Still, William N., Jr., ed., *The Confederate Navy, The Ships, Men and Organization, 1861-65*, London, Conway Maritime Press, p. 64.
23. Dudley, William S., *Going South, U.S. Navy Officer Resignations and Dismissals on the Eve of the Civil War*, Washington, p. 7, 19.
24. Still, op. cit p. 12.
25. Hearn, op cit. pgs. 21-23.
26. Still, op. cit. p. 52.
27. Hearn, op. cit. pgs. 204-205.
28. McAulay, op. cit. p. 135.
29. Still, op. cit. p. 64.
30. Hearn, op. cit. pgs. 174-178.
31. Faust, op. cit, p. 205.
32. Ibid, p. 9.
33. Still, op. cit. pgs. 204-205.
34. Ibid, pgs. 58-61.
35. Ripley, op. cit. pgs. 127-136.
36. Daniel, Larry J., and Gunter, Riley W., *Confederate Cannon Foundries*, Union City, TN, Pioneer Press, pgs. 75-84, 94-104.

Index

128